Romeo and Juliet
GCSE English Literature for AQA
Student Book

Chris Sutcliffe and Bernard Ward
with Lucien Jenkins and Rob Smith
Series editor: Peter Thomas

CAMBRIDGE
UNIVERSITY PRESS

University Printing House, Cambridge CB2 8BS, United Kingdom

Cambridge University Press is part of the University of Cambridge.

It furthers the University's mission by disseminating knowledge in the pursuit of
education, learning and research at the highest international levels of excellence.

www.cambridge.org
Information on this title: www.cambridge.org/9781107453821 (Paperback)
www.cambridge.org/9781107453883 (Cambridge Elevate-enhanced Edition)
www.cambridge.org/9781107453937 (Paperback + Cambridge Elevate-enhanced Edition)

© Cambridge University Press 2015

This publication is in copyright. Subject to statutory exception
and to the provisions of relevant collective licensing agreements,
no reproduction of any part may take place without the written
permission of Cambridge University Press.

First published 2015

Printed in Dubai by Oriental Press

A catalogue record for this publication is available from the British Library

ISBN 978-1-107-45382-1 Paperback
ISBN 978-1-107-45388-3 Cambridge Elevate-enhanced Edition
ISBN 978-1-107-45393-7 Paperback + Cambridge Elevate-enhanced Edition

Additional resources for this publication at www.cambridge.org/ukschools

Cambridge University Press has no responsibility for the persistence or accuracy
of URLs for external or third-party internet websites referred to in this publication,
and does not guarantee that any content on such websites is, or will remain,
accurate or appropriate. Information regarding prices, travel timetables, and other
factual information given in this work is correct at the time of first printing but
Cambridge University Press does not guarantee the accuracy of such information
thereafter.

....

NOTICE TO TEACHERS IN THE UK
It is illegal to reproduce any part of this work in material form (including
photocopying and electronic storage) except under the following circumstances:
(i)   where you are abiding by a licence granted to your school or institution by the
      Copyright Licensing Agency;
(ii) where no such licence exists, or where you wish to exceed the terms of a licence,
      and you have gained the written permission of Cambridge University Press;
(iii) where you are allowed to reproduce without permission under the provisions
      of Chapter 3 of the Copyright, Designs and Patents Act 1988, which covers, for
      example, the reproduction of short passages within certain types of educational
      anthology and reproduction for the purposes of setting examination questions.

Message from AQA

This textbook has been approved by AQA for use with our qualification. This means that we have checked that it
broadly covers the specification and we are satisfied with the overall quality. Full details of our approval process can be
found on our website.

We approve textbooks because we know how important it is for teachers and students to have the right resources
to support their teaching and learning. However, the publisher is ultimately responsible for the editorial control and
quality of this book.

Please note that when teaching the AQA GCSE English Literature (8702) course, you must refer to AQA's specification
as your definitive source of information. While this book has been written to match the specification, it cannot provide
complete coverage of every aspect of the course.

A wide range of other useful resources can be found on the relevant subject pages of our website: aqa.org.uk

Contents

Introduction

Welcome to your AQA GCSE English Literature student book on *Romeo and Juliet* – one of Shakespeare's best-known plays, and one that we hope you will enjoy at GCSE and later in life. Much of the play deals with things you are familiar with, and may even be an expert on – group rivalries, arguments with parents, love (rejected), love (fulfilled), and on-the-spot decisions that affect your life and the lives of those around you.

This book will help you make the most of the play and of your GCSE. It will develop your skills in reading and responding to a Shakespeare text, and in writing for GCSE English Literature.

The book is organised as follows:

Part 1: Exploring the play
Part 1 leads you through each act of the play. It ensures that you build an understanding of the action, dramatic structure and methods that Shakespeare uses to present his characters and ideas as a text to be performed in a theatre to the audiences of *Romeo and Juliet*. Each unit provides activities for discussion and drama-based approaches.

You will also develop your skills in writing about the play. Your work with each unit will result in notes and focused responses on aspects of the play that are important for GCSE. These will also be useful when you revise for your exam.

Part 2: The play as a whole
Part 2 provides an overview of key aspects of the play, including structure, contexts, characterisation and language. It will develop your knowledge and understanding, and also help you to revise your responses to the play as a whole.

On Cambridge Elevate you will find video clips that deepen your experience, understanding, interpretations and analysis of the play.

Preparing for your exam
This part gives you practice and guidance to help you prepare for your examination. It also provides examples of answers showing skills at different levels so you can assess where your skills are strong and where to focus your efforts to improve.

We hope that you will enjoy using these resources, not only to support your study, but to help you see that a Shakespeare play has plenty to say about life around you – and within you.

Peter Thomas
Series Editor

Introducing Romeo and Juliet

SHAKESPEARE AND *ROMEO AND JULIET*

William Shakespeare was born in 1564 and died in 1616. He wrote 38 plays (some say 39), which are usually divided into comedies, histories, tragedies and romances. However, it's important to understand that Shakespeare often mixed his ingredients, rather than following a formula. For instance the tragedies often contain a few comic characters and scenes.

Romeo and Juliet is one of Shakespeare's early plays. He probably wrote it in 1593 or 1594, when he was in his late twenties or early thirties. At this point, Shakespeare was making a name for himself as an upcoming writer, after spending several years as an actor.

It is unlike many of his other plays, as it reflects the plots, wars and political conflicts that he heard about as a boy and lived through as a man. It is the only play he wrote that has teenagers as the main characters. This was not because he was appealing to a teenage audience, but because he knew the story was a popular one that had been published in verse in 1562 and in prose in 1567. Shakespeare's knowledge of young people's lives and passions had a personal aspect: he married Anne Hathaway when he was only 18. She was 26, and already three months pregnant with their first daughter, Susannah.

Structure and plot

Romeo and Juliet contains five acts, each split into several scenes to vary the pace, mood, plot and characters. Act 1 establishes the main characters and the main action. Acts 2, 3 and 4 develop the action and the characters, and Act 5 brings the story to a conclusion. More importantly, the division into scenes keeps the audience engaged and interested as Shakespeare changes the setting from the streets of Verona to Juliet's bedroom to the Capulets' ballroom to Friar Lawrence's dwelling and eventually to a tomb. As the Friar concludes, **'Romeo, there dead, was husband to that Juliet, / And she, there dead, that Romeo's faithful wife'.**

The plot is a rapid sequence of meeting, secret marrying, desperate measures to get out of a planned marriage, and a double death at the end. Along the way, there are fights, deaths, punishments and cunning plans involving priests and chemists. Add some music, some dancing and some humour and there is enough variety in plot and structure to keep any audience watching and listening.

 Read about the action of *Romeo and Juliet* in this Introduction and find out more about the play's plot and structure in Unit 6.

If love be rough with you, be rough with love:
Prick love for pricking, and you beat love down.

Mercutio: Act 1 Scene 4, lines 27–28

Context and setting

You need to know something about life in Shakespeare's time – and especially what theatres and audiences were like. This is not a history task. You simply need to know that Shakespeare wrote for an audience that included many people who could not read or write. He also wrote for those who already knew the stories that he was turning into plays. The theatre he wrote for had none of the sound amplification, scenery, lighting or special effects that we have today. Shakespeare therefore had to make use of his audience's imagination.

There are other contexts of performance to consider, such as the different ways a scene may be performed on screen and on stage, or for an audience of children or adults. However, you mainly need to know about the contexts of writing and performing. You are studying *Romeo and Juliet* in the context of GCSE English Literature, which may be different from the context of watching it in the theatre.

When Shakespeare added to the sources he used, it was to create a wider social context for the young couple's actions. For instance the play includes the social context of Verona, with Capulet's plans for his daughter and his concern to arrange a marriage that was favourable to him as well as her.

Shakespeare also placed the story in the context of long-term rivalry and hostility between the Capulet family and the Montague family. This allowed him to include scenes of conflict between father and daughter, and scenes of public rivalry and disorder.

The other wider context is the supernatural one. Shakespeare presents Romeo and Juliet as '**star-crossed**' lovers, doomed to a tragic end by fate or fortune. This makes the play rather more complex because it is never clear whether their tragic ending is a result of their own rash, impatient deeds or due to the evil influence of destiny.

 Read more about the context and setting of *Romeo and Juliet* in Unit 7.

Characterisation

The main characters, Romeo and Juliet, are not as complex as the characters in Shakespeare's later tragedies – perhaps partly because they are young people, whose characters are not yet fully developed. In any case, at this early stage in his career, Shakespeare seems to have been more interested in writing plays with strong plots, rather than complex characters.

Other characters provide variety and contrast around the main characters. For instance Benvolio has a down-to-earth sensible attitude, in contrast to Romeo's over-romantic and passionate feelings. Tybalt provides a fiery-tempered masculine sense of honour, in contrast to Romeo's sensitive and private nature. The Nurse provides comic relief in her manner of speaking. She tells Romeo that her mistress was once '**a little prating thing**' and Juliet would rather see '**a toad**' than Paris. Mercutio also provides a lighter tone with his rude jokes: '**If love be rough with you, be rough with love: / Prick love for pricking, and you beat love down.**'

Read about the characters in *Romeo and Juliet* in this Introduction and find out more about characterisation in the play in Unit 8.

The ideas in the play

Themes are the subjects that literature is based on. As in Shakespeare's day, some of the most common themes in books and plays are still love and hate in relationships, reactions to events large and small, and human characteristics such as passion, doubt, fear, success and failure.

Ideas are ways of understanding aspects of the themes. Ideas about love can vary a great deal. For instance a writer may want to express the idea that love makes the world and people better, or that it makes them insecure and jealous, or that it doesn't last, or that it helps people through difficulties.

In the same way, a writer may want to show different ideas about war – that it brings out the best or the worst in people, or that it is sadly necessary in order to defend something important, or that it is a tragic waste because it is not really necessary.

The main idea in *Romeo and Juliet* is that extremes of passion can lead to complications and choices that may not be what was expected – and may lead to tragic consequences. However, Shakespeare includes the idea that external causes can influence human destiny – in this case, he suggests the influence of the supernatural, in the form of fate, which has already marked the two young lovers down for disaster.

Read more about the ideas in *Romeo and Juliet* in Unit 9.

Language

Apart from all his other talents, Shakespeare's greatest gift is his use of the English language to write speeches that convey a range of passions. He can also realistically portray all types of people: peasants, soldiers, lords and ladies, or bishops, clowns and people who serve in pubs. To do this, he has to make an audience imagine what he can't show them on stage and use images drawn from trades, household life and sport to make ideas seem familiar.

... my mistress is the sweetest lady – Lord, Lord! when 'twas a little prating thing ...

Nurse: Act 2 Scene 4, lines 167–168

For example Romeo's first meeting with Juliet is written in language that mixes physical love and religious worship. Shakespeare uses the audience's knowledge of religious pilgrimages (journeys to famous religious sites) to represent Romeo's love as not just physical attraction but also something similar to worshipping a goddess:

> If I profane with my unworthiest hand
> This holy shrine, the gentle sin is this,
> My lips, two blushing pilgrims, ready stand
> To smooth that rough touch with a tender kiss.

Romeo: Act 1 Scene 5, lines 92-95

 Read more about the language of *Romeo and Juliet* in Unit 10.

Interpretation and performance

Your own response to the play matters – what you think of the characters, which scenes make you laugh or feel sad. Most importantly, you need to consider what Shakespeare's plays mean to you when they show you ways that people behave, and how relationships can develop or go wrong.

Interpretation can be personal to you, or related to all people, or to some people.

For example some would see Juliet as disrespectful of her father and mother and irresponsible in rushing into a secret marriage with someone she's only just met. Others may see her as a strong-minded youngster who knows what she wants and is too independent to allow her parents to decide who she can marry.

Drama is public entertainment. Whether on stage or screen, or in your classroom, you will get closest to Shakespeare when you see the text turning into action. This is when your understanding of plot and character, themes and ideas, language, stagecraft and theatricality will come together, because interpretation and performance are what the text is all about. Connecting the words with what actors have done with them, or with what you think actors **could** do with them, will ensure that you write about Shakespeare as a dramatist.

If I profane with my unworthiest hand
This holy shrine ...

Romeo: Act 1 Scene 5, lines 92-93

SHAKESPEARE AND GCSE ENGLISH LITERATURE

Your GCSE course has been designed so that you experience a range of drama, prose and poetry texts from the last few hundred years of English Literature. The point of this range is to help you understand that some things change over time – and some things don't. One of the most useful ways of exploring ideas in the play is to ask, 'Is this about events and characters long gone, or is it about something that we can still see and experience today?' This question opens up major issues of relevance, context and Shakespeare's value as a writer.

At the end of your GCSE course in English Literature you will sit an exam. The Literature exam has two papers:

- **Paper 1 Shakespeare and the 19th-century novel,** which is worth 40% of your GCSE
- **Paper 2 Modern texts and poetry**, which is worth 60% of your GCSE.

SHAKESPEARE IN THE EXAM

Paper 1 Shakespeare and the 19th-century novel has two sections:

- **Section A Shakespeare**, where you answer one question on the play of your choice – *Romeo and Juliet* in this case. You will be required to write in detail about an extract from the play and then to write about the play as a whole.
- **Section B The 19th-century novel**, where you answer one question on the novel of your choice. You will be required to write in detail about an extract from the novel and then to write about the novel as a whole.

GCSE ENGLISH LITERATURE ASSESSMENT OBJECTIVES

The assessment objectives (AOs) form the basis for the GCSE mark scheme. Your study of the play will be assessed by an examiner who will be looking for your skill in writing about what the play is about and how it is written. For Paper 1, Section A, you will be assessed on four AOs:

Assessment objective 1

Read, understand and respond to texts. Students should be able to:

- maintain a critical style and develop an informed personal response
- use textual references, including quotations, to support and illustrate interpretations.

Assessment objective 2

Analyse the language, form and structure used by a writer to create meanings and effects, using relevant subject terminology where appropriate.

Assessment objective 3

Show understanding of the relationships between texts and the contexts in which they were written. (These 'contexts' may include also the context in which a text is set, literary contexts such as genres, and the context of different audiences – including you in the 21st century.)

Assessment objective 4

Use a range of vocabulary and sentence structures for clarity, purpose and effect, with accurate spelling and punctuation.

Good night, good night! Parting is such sweet sorrow,
That I shall say good night till it be morrow.

Juliet: Act 2 Scene 2, lines 184–185

LITERATURE SKILLS AND STUDY FOCUS AREAS

Most of your study will be based on reading the text, but this will not be enough if you are to understand and enjoy the play as drama. The text doesn't become drama until it is performed, and actors bring the words to life. You should therefore make sure that you **see** the play, and connect the words on the page with performance on stage or screen.

Most of the skills you develop in your literature study will be the same as those in other parts of your GCSE English reading. You will develop your core skills to show **understanding**, **interpretation** and **analysis**. We will explore these skills, along with the following study focus areas, in this book.

Ideas, attitudes and feelings

These amount to **content** – what's in the play. The important thing to remember is that they are three different things.

- **Ideas** are the thoughts that explain or result from an experience.
- **Attitudes** are the positions or postures we adopt when facing experiences
- **Feelings** are the emotions people feel, which are often quite different from their attitudes and ideas.

For example you could say that:

- An **idea** is that romantic love is a more powerful emotion than feelings for family.
- An **attitude** is that falling in love with one woman is weakness and it makes sense to '**examine other beauties**'.
- A **feeling** is that '**parting is such sweet sorrow**'.

The writer's methods

You will be expected to understand and respond to the feelings, ideas or attitudes expressed in the play, and also to understand and respond to the way the play is written – the writer's methods. These amount to language, form and structure. The important thing to remember is that they are three different things.

For example you could say that:

- The **language** is written to help actors speak their lines and to convey ideas and feelings through imagery.
- The **form** is a five-act play, with each act divided into scenes.
- The **structure** is based on Romeo and Juliet's progress, from first meeting to secret marriage to tragic outcome.

DEVELOPING WRITTEN RESPONSE SKILLS

This book supports you in writing that is focused on the GCSE study areas. It helps you to identify where your skills are strong and what you need to do to improve.

You will move from the ability to make 'basic' comments that are relevant (including a quotation to support the comment) to using your understanding and interpretation skills to explain feelings, motives or reasons, presenting ideas that develop and extend meaning. For example:

Juliet doesn't want Romeo to leave her in the morning so she says 'it was the nightingale and not the lark' that they heard.

> shows a relevant response, supported with quotation

Juliet shows her love for Romeo by trying to make him stay as long as possible, even when they have heard the lark's singing as a sign that it is morning, and he has to go in case her parents find him there. She tries to persuade him that it was the nightingale, so it must be still night, and they have plenty of time left together before he has to go.

> shows understanding with clear explanation

Shakespeare creates a sense of passion and humour in these lines. Juliet's passion shows because she wants Romeo to stay as long as possible, even though she knows he risks death if he is found in her bedroom. When they hear the lark, proving that it is morning, she tries to persuade him that it is the nightingale, and that they still have time together. The humour comes from Romeo teasing her by saying that he believes her and will stay, even if it means he gets killed, which then makes her change her mind.

> shows exploration and evaluation

Writing with focus

This book also develops focused writing so that you can be ready and confident when writing in timed conditions in the exam. Be prepared to show how Shakespeare builds the play as a theatrical experience, appealing to a wide range of audiences. Demonstrate how he uses his writer's craft to set the scene in an exciting way, to use characters as a mouthpiece for his ideas, and to work on audience sympathies and fears in order to build suspense.

When you respond to a question on the play, you need to show that your response is dealing with essential GCSE skills, and linked to specific details of the text, making your points quickly and linking your chosen textual detail to a clear purpose.

THE ACTION OF *ROMEO AND JULIET*

Prologue

The Chorus describes the play: the death of two young lovers (Romeo Montague and Juliet Capulet) will end the bitter conflict between their violently feuding families.

Act 1

Two Capulet servants pick a fight with two Montague servants. Tybalt (a Capulet) arrives. Benvolio (a Montague) tries to make peace but a riot starts. Lord Capulet and Lord Montague appear and join in. Prince Escales stops the brawl and threatens death to Montague and Capulet if they fight in public again.

Romeo tells Benvolio he's been quiet recently because he's in love with a woman who doesn't love him back.

Paris wants to marry Juliet (who is only thirteen), and discusses it with her father. Capulet invites Paris to his masked ball. Meanwhile Romeo decides to gatecrash the same party after discovering that Rosaline, the woman he is in love with, is on the guest list.

Lady Capulet, the Nurse and Juliet chat about Juliet's marriage prospects. Lady Capulet can't say enough good things about Count Paris.

Romeo and his friends prepare for Capulet's party. Mercutio describes Queen Mab, the bewitching queen of the fairies.

Everyone at Capulet's house has been preparing for the ball. When Romeo arrives, he catches sight of Juliet, and is entranced. Tybalt is furious when he discovers that Romeo has dared to sneak in. Romeo and Juliet meet and fall in love at first sight. The Nurse calls Juliet away, and Romeo learns that she is a member of the Capulet family.

Act 2

Romeo has broken away from his friends. He sees Juliet at a window, but she hasn't seen him. She talks aloud about how she hates the fact that their families are deadly enemies. Romeo calls up to her, and they declare their love for one another. They decide to get married, and Juliet says she will send a messenger the next day to find out when and where. Romeo leaves to make plans.

Friar Lawrence is gathering herbs at dawn when Romeo arrives at the Friar's cell (dwelling). Romeo asks the Friar to marry him and Juliet. The Friar tells Romeo off for falling in love so quickly again, but agrees to the marriage because he believes that it will end the Montague and Capulet feud.

Mercutio teases Romeo about Rosaline. The Nurse appears as Juliet's messenger, and Mercutio teases her too. Romeo tells the Nurse to bring Juliet to Friar Lawrence's cell that afternoon.

Juliet waits eagerly for the Nurse to return with news. When she finally arrives, grumbling about her aches and pains, she takes her time to reveal the plan.

Romeo and the Friar wait for Juliet. When Juliet arrives, the couple hurry away to be married.

Act 3

Benvolio is worried about the rising tension between the Montagues and Capulets, but Mercutio laughs it off. Tybalt enters, wanting to challenge Romeo to a duel. Romeo, newly married to Juliet, tries to make peace. Mercutio, frustrated, challenges Tybalt himself. Romeo tries to stop the fight and steps between them, but in the confusion Tybalt kills Mercutio. Romeo blames himself, but kills Tybalt. The Prince banishes Romeo from Verona on pain of death.

In her bedroom, Juliet is waiting for Romeo, unaware of what's happened. The Nurse arrives and tells her the news. Juliet threatens to kill herself, but the Nurse promises to send Romeo to her.

Romeo is hiding in Friar Lawrence's cell. He might as well be dead, he says, as life is only worth living with Juliet in Verona. The Nurse arrives and the Friar works out a plan: Romeo should spend the night with Juliet, then leave early in the morning for Mantua. Once the Capulets and Montagues have stopped fighting, Romeo can return.

Lord Capulet has decided to marry Juliet to Paris. He asks his wife to tell Juliet that the wedding will take place in three days' time.

In her bedroom, Juliet tries to persuade Romeo not to leave. As Lady Capulet approaches, the two lovers say goodbye. Juliet flatly refuses to marry Paris. Her father comes in and flies into a rage. Coming close to physical violence, he threatens to disown her and storms out. Juliet's mother refuses to help, and the Nurse advises Juliet to marry Paris. Left alone, Juliet decides to ask Friar Lawrence for help, but plans to kill herself as a last resort.

Act 4

Juliet begs the Friar for help. He suggests a desperate plan: she must agree to marry Paris, but then drink a potion that will make her appear to be dead. The Friar will call Romeo back from Mantua and he will rescue her from the Capulet tomb. She instantly accepts this plan.

Capulet delightedly prepares for a grand wedding. Meanwhile, in her bedroom, Juliet plucks up the courage to drink the potion.

The wedding preparations are under way when Juliet is discovered 'dead' by her family. Friar Lawrence reassures them that Juliet is now in a better place in Heaven.

Act 5

In Mantua, Romeo describes a dream he had in which Juliet found him dead but revived him with kisses. His servant Balthasar brings dreadful news from Verona: Juliet is dead. Romeo resolves to kill himself that night in the tomb with Juliet. He buys poison from an apothecary (pharmacist) and leaves for Verona.

Meanwhile, the Friar has sent a letter explaining the deception to Romeo, but he discovers that his letter never reached Romeo. Alarmed, he decides to break into Juliet's tomb to be with her when she wakes.

Paris is visiting Juliet's tomb to mourn. He hides when Romeo and Balthasar appear. Romeo tells Balthasar to leave, but Balthasar hides and watches. Paris tries to stop Romeo from breaking into the tomb. They fight and Romeo ends up killing Paris. Romeo lays Paris next to Juliet inside the tomb. He drinks the poison, kisses Juliet, and dies.

Friar Lawrence arrives just as Juliet wakes up, asking for Romeo. He urges her to come away, but leaves in a hurry when he hears the Watch (night watchmen). Seeing Romeo dead, Juliet looks for any last drops of poison in the bottle or on Romeo's lips; finding none, she kills herself with Romeo's dagger.

All the remaining characters arrive. The Prince promises to punish the culprits, and Montague and Capulet promise to end their feud.

THE MAIN CHARACTERS IN *ROMEO AND JULIET*

Juliet is the young daughter of Lord and Lady Capulet.

Capulet is Juliet's father, a wealthy nobleman in the city of Verona.

Lady Capulet is Juliet's mother.

Tybalt is Juliet's cousin.

Romeo is the son of Lord and Lady Montague.

Benvolio is Romeo's friend.

Balthasar is Romeo's servant.

Prince Escales is the ruler of Verona.

Mercutio is related to the Prince and he is Romeo's friend.

Paris is also related to the Prince and he wants to marry Juliet.

Friar Lawrence is a Franciscan priest.

1

Act 1: Prospects and problems

How does Shakespeare open the play in Act 1?

Your progress in this unit:

- understand Shakespeare's decision about how to open the play
- explain the way Shakespeare establishes character
- explore Shakespeare's ideas in the play, and the social and political context
- analyse Shakespeare's use of language, form and structure
- develop your written response skills.

GETTING STARTED - THE PLAY AND YOU

Thinking about the opening of the play

Romeo and Juliet is one of Shakespeare's best-loved and most frequently performed plays. The famous story of star-crossed lovers (with its **themes** of youthful romance, teenage rebellion and violent conflict between social groups) remains as relevant in the 21st century as it was at the end of the 16th century.

 What do you already know about the play *Romeo and Juliet*? How would you introduce it to someone who hasn't seen it?

2 The action of the play starts with a fight. If you are in a situation where there is an argument, do you:

a   jump into the middle of it without thinking?

b   have doubts about getting involved and hang back?

c   try to act as peacemaker?

Watch a three-minute summary of the play on Cambridge Elevate.

GETTING CLOSER - FOCUS ON DETAILS

How does Shakespeare use Act 1 to get the audience involved?

Act 1 (in a play of five acts) is mostly about setting up the play. In Act 1 of *Romeo and Juliet*, Shakespeare wants to establish the basic outline of the plot and the characters, and also the atmosphere and the main ideas.

Most importantly, he wants to engage his audience through his use of language and dramatic devices. Read through the key details for each scene in the flow diagram, to get an overview of Act 1.

1 In groups, read the plot summary and discuss what is being 'established' in Act 1.

a   Then, on your own, write a short (50- to 100-word) trailer for a new film of *Romeo and Juliet*.

b   Concentrate only on information about Act 1 and try to use key details and words from the text to grab the audience's attention and make them want to see it.

c   Compare your trailer with those produced by some other members of your group.

 Key terms

theme: an idea or concept that recurs throughout a play.

Prologue
The Chorus introduces the play, describing the conflict between the Montague and Capulet families and the fate of the lovers, Romeo and Juliet.

Scene 1
Servants of the Montague family fight with servants of the Capulet family. The audience sees the enmity between Lord Capulet and Lord Montague, and how Prince Escales breaks up the fight. Romeo is introduced. He's in low spirits because he's in love with Rosaline, but she's not interested.

Scene 2
Lord Capulet is talking to Paris, who wishes to marry Juliet and will woo her at the masked ball that evening. Romeo and Benvolio hear about the ball and decide to go.

Scene 3
Lady Capulet tells Juliet and her Nurse (who has looked after Juliet since she was a baby) that there are plans for Juliet to marry Paris.

Scene 4
Romeo, Benvolio and Mercutio are outside the Capulet mansion, where the ball is taking place. Mercutio tries to persuade Romeo to cheer up, forget Rosaline and go to the ball.

Scene 5
At the ball, Romeo is overwhelmed by Juliet's beauty: **'O she doth teach the torches to burn bright!'** They meet and fall in love. There is almost another fight between the warring families when Tybalt spots Romeo, but Lord Capulet stops him. Later, Juliet learns from her Nurse that Romeo is a Montague. Even so, she realises that she loves him.

PROLOGUE AND ACT 1 SCENE 1: MAJOR AND MINOR CHARACTERS

Shakespeare's use of fate in the Prologue

Shakespeare introduces the play with a Prologue, which tells the audience what is going to happen. Spoiler alert! *Romeo and Juliet* is a story where the audience already knows the ending: the lovers die. (It's rather like the film *Titanic*, where everyone knows the ship is going to sink.)

1 Put these statements in rank order according to how convincing you think they are, and explain your decisions:

A People will watch in case there is a surprise ending after all.

B People will watch because they are fans of the actors.

C People will watch because there will be exciting special effects.

D People will watch because they will be emotionally involved in the story.

E People will watch because they know the ending but the characters don't.

2 Look again at the Prologue. How do you know that:

a the hatred between the two families has been going on for a long time

b their hatred has turned Verona into a war zone

c the two young people will fall in love

d their love will end in death for both of them

e there is nothing they can do to stop this, as it is all fated to happen?

3 Use a table like this one to list the similarities between the Montagues and the Capulets, as described in the Prologue. Two examples have been done for you. What other details can you find?

What details suggest that the two families have things in common at the start of the play?	In line 1 we are told that both families are '**alike in dignity**' (they are both equal in their high social status).
What details suggest that the two families will have things in common by the end of the play?	In line 8 the Chorus explains that Romeo and Juliet's deaths will 'bury their parents' strife' (put an end to their fighting).

A pair of star-crossed lovers take their life;
Whose misadventured piteous overthrows
Doth with their death bury their parents' strife.

Chorus: The Prologue, lines 6–8

4 Work in pairs. Think of an idea for a photograph to illustrate each of the following phrases from the Prologue. Make notes on each one.

    a   **Two households**
    b   **From ancient grudge break to new mutiny**
    c   **A pair of star-crossed lovers take their life**
    d   **Doth with their death bury their parents' strife**
    e   **The fearful passage of their death-marked love**
    f   **Is now the two hours' traffic of our stage**
    g   **The which if you with patient ears attend**

 Now watch a video of actors doing this task on Cambridge Elevate.

Minor characters

Following the Prologue, Shakespeare opens Scene 1 with a conversation between two minor characters, Sampson and Gregory.

1 Look at Sampson and Gregory's conversation in lines 1–30.

    a   Choose two words from the word bank to describe their **dialogue**.

witty	intelligent	aggressive
bigoted	boastful	crude

> 🔑 **Key terms**
>
> **dialogue:** a conversation between two or more people in a piece of writing.

    b   Find a quotation from their dialogue to support each of your choices.

2 The comic chat between Sampson and Gregory is followed by an argument, which leads to a fight.

    a   Look at lines 28–63. What examples can you find of language used in a way that expresses anger or causes offence?
    b   In a group, choose two lines or phrases from this part of the scene that you think would be most likely to start a fight.

 **Contexts**

Shakespeare's audience was partly made up of young boys who were learning a trade. They were known as apprentices and often caused trouble on London streets. Some critics have argued that the rude jokes in *Romeo and Juliet* were put in to please the apprentices, while the lords and ladies enjoyed the poetic speeches in the play. However, it's quite possible that the apprentices also enjoyed poetry, and that lords and ladies laughed at the rude bits as much as anyone else.

Major characters

Shakespeare introduces several major characters in this first scene: Lord Montague, Lord and Lady Capulet, Romeo and Benvolio. Shakespeare uses them to show certain attitudes, which may change during the play.

Characterisation is the art of making a character believable. Writers establish characters in three key ways, through:

- **what they say** (their language, vocabulary and the images they use)
- **what they do** (their actions, their reactions to events and their expressions of feeling)
- **how others respond to them or speak about them** (the language used to describe them and how people act or behave in their presence).

When exploring character, certain incidents offer useful evidence. When one character responds to, or speaks about another, you may learn something about both of them. An example is shown in this flow diagram.

> **What Benvolio does**
> Although a friend of the Montague household, he does not take sides in the brawl, but attempts to come between the fighting servants.

⬇

> **What Benvolio says to Tybalt** (lines 59–60)
> 'I do but keep the peace. Put up thy sword, Or manage it to part these men with me.'

⬇

> **How Tybalt responds to Benvolio** (line 63)
> Tybalt calls him '**coward**' and attacks him.

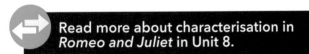

Read more about characterisation in _Romeo and Juliet_ in Unit 8.

1 In pairs, discuss how this incident gives a sense of Benvolio's character.

2 What do you learn about Tybalt from this encounter?

3 Create a similar flow diagram for Lord Montague. Compare his brief dialogue with his wife (lines 70–71) to his conversation with Benvolio (lines 145–8). What two sides of his character do these dialogues reveal?

Although the Prince is a minor character, he is the ruler of Verona and represents law and order. He is important in this scene because he stops the fighting that has broken out and makes it clear that any future rioting will lead to the death penalty.

4 Read lines 72–95. Imagine you are a director who is rehearsing this speech with the actor playing the Prince. The Prince has asked you to explain some of the phrases and how they might be delivered to best effect. The first phrase has been done for you as an example.

What ho! you men, you beasts!
That quench the fire of your pernicious rage
With purple fountains issuing from your veins:

Prince: Act 1 Scene 1, lines 74–76

The Prince expresses his anger by shouting 'What, ho!' to get the attention of his subjects. He is annoyed at the brutality of their fighting, describing them as 'beasts' rather than civilised men. As a figure of authority and power, his language is suitably impressive and elaborate. The Prince describes the rioters' rage as 'pernicious' (wicked); their blood is like 'purple fountains'. It is important to him to express his status by using such grand terms.

Choose one of these quotations and think about what you might say.

On pain of torture, from those bloody hands
Throw your mistempered weapons to the ground,
And hear the sentence of your movèd prince.

Prince: Act 1 Scene 1, lines 77–79

Three civil brawls, bred of an airy word,
By thee, old Capulet, and Montague,
Have thrice disturbed the quiet of our streets …

Prince: Act 1 Scene 1, lines 80–82

 Watch the Prince's speech on Cambridge Elevate.

Form and structure of language

Shakespeare also varies the form of his language. In this scene, he uses **prose** for the servants, **blank verse** (which is usually written in **iambic pentameter**) for the Prince, and rhymed **verse** for the dialogue of Benvolio and Romeo. Here is an example of the Prince's speech:

If ever you disturb our streets again,
Your lives shall pay the forfeit of the peace.

Prince: Act 1 Scene 1, lines 87–88

In Act 1, Scene 1, lines 208–209, Romeo and Benvolio share rhymes:

Benvolio: Then she hath sworn that she will still live chaste?
Romeo: She hath, and in that sparing makes huge waste:

1 Can you suggest one possible reason why Shakespeare does this with Romeo and Benvolio's language?

2 Where does Scene 1 change between prose, blank verse and rhymed verse?

3 Look at what is happening at those moments and what the characters talk about. Why might Shakespeare have made those changes?

 Key terms

characterisation: the way a writer paints a picture of a particular character, through their words, actions and reactions.

prose: writing that follows the style of normal speech.

blank verse: unrhymed verse with carefully placed stressed and unstressed syllables.

iambic pentameter: the rhythm created by a line of ten syllables with five stressed syllables.

verse: writing that has a particular rhyme, pattern or rhythm.

If ever you disturb our streets again,
Your lives shall pay the forfeit of the peace.

Prince: Act 1 Scene 1, lines 87–88

> Take thou some new infection to thy eye,
> And the rank poison of the old will die.

Benvolio: Act 1 Scene 2, lines 48-49

ACT I SCENES 2 AND 3: CONTEXT, LANGUAGE AND RELATIONSHIPS

Context and language in Act 1 Scene 2

1 Look at this table, comparing family life in Shakespeare's England with family life in modern Britain.

In Shakespeare's Tudor England	In most families in modern Britain
Prosperous parents arrange their child's marriage.	Adult children choose their own marriage partners.
Thirteen-year-old girls get married and have children.	The minimum age for sexual relations and marriage is 16.
Families usually include two parents.	One-parent families are common.
Girls only inherit their parents' estate if they have no brothers.	Girls and boys have an equal right to inherit their parents' estate.

a Which of the statements in the left-hand column might a 21st-century British audience find most shocking?

b Which of the statements in the right-hand column might a 16th-century English audience find most shocking?

2 How far does Shakespeare present Lord Capulet as:

a a caring parent who wants the best for his daughter

b a father who regards his daughter as his property?

This scene begins with Lord Capulet and Paris discussing Paris's wish to marry Juliet. Juliet's father stresses that his daughter is still only thirteen but says he will approve the marriage if Juliet also agrees. Benvolio enters and talks persuasively to Romeo about love. Benvolio uses two related images:

> Take thou some new <u>infection</u> to thy eye.
> And the rank <u>poison</u> of the old will die.

Benvolio: Act 1 Scene 2, lines 48-49

3 Read Benvolio's lines carefully.

a What is Benvolio advising Romeo to do?

b What does Benvolio's choice of **imagery** tell you about his attitude to relationships?

c What are the **connotations** of these images? Relate the connotations to the themes established in the Prologue, and developed in the Prince's warning to the troublemakers in Scene 1. What do the connotations suggest about the dangers of love for Romeo?

 Key terms

imagery: language intended to conjure up a vivid picture in the reader or audience's mind.

connotation: an idea or a feeling linked to the main meaning of a word – what it implies or suggests in addition to its literal meaning.

Earlier in the scene she refers to Juliet as 'lamb' and 'ladybird'. The Nurse is clearly showing warmth and affection for Juliet.

1 How typical is this of the way that she treats Juliet in the rest of the scene?

In comparison in lines 70–75, Lady Capulet says:

Well, think of marriage now; younger than you,
Here in Verona, ladies of esteem,
Are made already mothers. By my count,
I was your mother much upon these years
That you are now a maid. Thus then in brief:
The valiant Paris seeks you for his love.

2 Notice that Juliet's mother seems less concerned with Juliet as a person and more intent on arranging for her an appropriately high-status husband ('**valiant Paris**'). This will allow her to become a mother at a very young age.

a   Read quickly through the Nurse and Lady Capulet's lines in the rest of this scene. As you do so, pay close attention to what the two women have to say about Juliet's childhood and about marriage.
b   On the basis of your enquiry, which character do you think shows greater understanding of Juliet and her situation?

Learning checkpoint

To improve your discussion of language, you should move from explaining to examining, and from examining to analysing.

✔ **Explain:** say what words mean; offer reasons for the writer's choice of words or imagery.
✔ **Examine:** look at the connotations and effects of particular words; relate them to the writer's purpose.
✔ **Analyse**: focus on specific words and images; suggest a range of possible connotations and effects.

The relationships in Act 1 Scene 3

Scene 3 includes three women (and a male servant, who appears briefly at the end). Shakespeare shows us a lot about the women's personalities and their relationships with each other:

• Lady Capulet asks a question and issues an order all in one line
• The nurse is talkative and humorous
• Juliet is polite and obedient.

In lines 61–63 the Nurse says:

Thou wast the prettiest babe that e'er I nursed.
And I might live to see thee married once,
I have my wish.

Well, think of marriage now; younger than you,
Here in Verona, ladies of esteem,
Are made already mothers.

Lady Capulet: Act 1 Scene 3, lines 70–72

21

> If thou art Dun we'll draw thee from the mire,
> Or (save your reverence) love, wherein thou stickest
> Up to the ears.

Mercutio: Act 1 Scene 4, lines 41–43

ACT 1 SCENES 4 AND 5: CHARACTER, LANGUAGE AND SETTING

Character and language in Act 1 Scene 4

In Scene 4 the action returns to Romeo and Mercutio, who are meeting outside the Capulet mansion (lines 44–101). Earlier (in Scene 2) Benvolio tried to convince Romeo to forget Rosaline and look at other girls. In Scene 4 Mercutio tries to convince him to forget love altogether, and have a good time.

1 We've already seen Romeo with Benvolio. Now we see him with another, very different friend.

a   What three words sum up your initial impression of Mercutio? Find evidence to support your response.

b   How is Mercutio's response to Romeo's troubles different from Benvolio's in Scene 2?

c   Romeo's reaction to Mercutio at lines 95–6, **'Peace, peace, Mercutio, peace! / Thou talk'st of nothing'** (Be quiet, Mercutio, you're talking nonsense), echoes Juliet's reaction to the Nurse in the previous scene (Scene 3 line 59). Why does Romeo choose to interrupt Mercutio at that precise moment? What does Mercutio say that seems to spark Romeo's response?

 Watch a discussion about Mercutio's character on Cambridge Elevate.

2 Now read the following lines closely:

> If thou art Dun we'll draw thee from the mire,
> Or (save your reverence) love, wherein thou stickest
> Up to the ears.

Mercutio: Act 1 Scene 4, lines 41–43

a   What do you think Mercutio means by **'save your reverence'**?

b   What is implied by his use of the word **'mire'** to describe love?

a   What does this add to the impression created by Benvolio's use of the words **'infection'** and **'poison'** to describe physical attraction in Scene 2?

Setting and context in Act 1 Scene 5

 Contexts

Masked balls were popular in Elizabethan Italy but some people disapproved of them because they thought wearing disguises encouraged immoral behaviour. (This was probably true. Perhaps it also helped to explain the popularity of these events!)

 Read more about language in *Romeo and Juliet* in Unit 10.

1 Scene 5 returns to a masked ball at the Capulets' mansion. Romeo sees Juliet and is amazed by her beauty; they speak, and then kiss.

a How has the atmosphere of the setting changed from Scenes 2–3?
b How might the party atmosphere account for the characters' behaviour?
c How might the fact that the partygoers are masked influence their actions?

2 Romeo and Juliet speak for the first time in lines 92–109. Look at the language they are using. What do you notice about the rhyming pattern of lines 92–105? These 14 lines (92–105) make up a **sonnet**, which has a distinctive **rhyme scheme**.

a To understand the literal meaning of Romeo's words in this passage, write it out as plain modern English sentences (prose). The first part of Romeo's speech (lines 92–93) has been modelled for you:

Romeo: If I profane with my unworthiest hand
This holy shrine …

Modern English:

'Your hands are like a sacred place of worship. If I touch them with my unworthy hands I might dishonour them … '

b Notice that Romeo uses words connected with religion such as '**profane**' and '**holy shrine**'. Can you trace a pattern of such words through the lovers' exchange?

Listen to a performance of this scene on Cambridge Elevate.

3 What does Juliet's role in this exchange tell you about her personality and her attitude to Romeo?

4 Read her speech carefully.

a Make a note of the positive and negative words she uses.

For example when Juliet says '**Ay, pilgrim, lips that they must use in prayer**', she might well be suggesting that lips are for speaking religious language rather than for kissing a young man who has just appeared!

b Look carefully at all the other words she uses when speaking to Romeo, and decide whether you think they are meant to encourage his attentions or not. You may find that it's not quite so obvious in all cases.

5 Imagine that you are directing a modern performance of *Romeo and Juliet*. Think about how you would stage this scene. You will need to consider:

a where you would set the scene
b how Romeo suddenly notices Juliet in the hustle and bustle of the dance and music
c how, and where, they talk to each other without being noticed by the other people
d how you would stage their first, dramatic kiss.

Work in a group and discuss how you would do this.

Watch actors and a director discuss this scene on Cambridge Elevate.

Key terms

sonnet: a verse form that English poets liked to use during the 16th century, especially when writing about love. It is a poem of 14 lines.
rhyme scheme: the pattern of a poem's rhyme, often identified by letters such as ABAB.

GETTING IT INTO WRITING

Writing about Shakespeare's use of language

The meeting of Romeo and Juliet is the climax of Act 1. Below are examples of three student responses to this part of the play. Each has been highlighted and annotated to show a key writing skill – writing about language.

RESPONSE 1

Romeo meets Juliet at the Capulets' party. He tries to chat her up by saying: 'If I profane with my unworthiest hand / This holy shrine'. <u>This shows that he is holding her hand</u>. Then he says: 'My lips, two blushing pilgrims, ready stand / To smooth that rough touch with a tender kiss'. <u>This tells us that he wants to kiss her hand</u>. Juliet says he is a 'Good pilgrim' and 'you do wrong your hand too much'. <u>This shows that she doesn't mind him touching her hand</u>. I reckon he kisses her hand, although it doesn't say so. Then he talks her into letting him kiss her on the lips. I know this because it says 'he kisses her'. <u>This shows that Romeo is very persuasive</u>.

> explains the literal meaning

> explains the literal meaning

> explains the literal meaning

> explains effect

RESPONSE 2

Romeo is trying to persuade Juliet to let him kiss her. He starts off by touching her hand. This is because he hopes she will let him kiss her hand. <u>I know this because he says</u>: 'My lips, two blushing pilgrims, ready stand / To smooth that rough touch with a tender kiss'. He calls her hand a 'holy shrine'. <u>This makes it seem like it's really important to Romeo and he doesn't feel worthy to touch it</u>. He hopes she will then let him kiss her on the lips. I think Romeo is very clever in the way he shows this, almost like he tricks Juliet because he says 'Have not saints lips?' <u>He is calling Juliet a saint, which implies that she is an object of worship to him, but he's saying that he's interested in her lips not just her palm</u>. Not only does Romeo call Juliet a saint, Juliet calls Romeo 'Good pilgrim'. <u>A pilgrim is someone who would travel to a shrine, so this is suggesting that she doesn't mind being touched by Romeo because the word 'pilgrim' has positive connotations, of someone whose motives are pure. This is reinforced by the fact that she says 'good' pilgrim. That's why she lets him kiss her</u>.

> explains the literal meaning

> begins to explore connotation

> more confident exploration

> confident exploration; beginning to analyse

If I profane with my unworthiest hand
This holy shrine ...

Romeo: Act 1 Scene 5, lines 92-93

RESPONSE 3

To start off with, Juliet seems not to be very interested because <u>she responds to Romeo in a joking way</u>. When he says that he will smooth his rough touch with a kiss she responds by saying, 'palm to palm is holy palmer's kiss'. <u>She seems to be saying that his touch is all she wants, and there is no need for him to kiss her hand.</u> <u>The use of the word 'holy' is interesting because we don't normally associate a meeting of lovers with the idea of something being sacred. There is a lot of religious language like this in their conversation</u>, which tells us a lot about the time Shakespeare was writing about, when religious beliefs were very important. Unlike for modern teenagers, for Romeo and Juliet becoming lovers was something they had to think about from this point of view, as well as worrying about the wishes of their parents. We can see this too in the way Romeo and Juliet both talk about 'sin' which means wrongdoing, almost as if they worry that what they are doing is wrong, but they can't help it because they are falling in love. This is shown by the fact that although Juliet is uncertain at the start, she is persuaded by Romeo and allows him to kiss her lips; love makes what is 'sinful' seem 'holy'.

| explains language use |
| develops exploration into analysis |
| explores connotation |
| develops exploration into analysis |

Now, using the work you have done in this unit, write a response of around 300 words to the following question:

Complete this assignment on Cambridge Elevate.

How does Shakespeare use language in the Prince's address to his subjects (Act 1 Scene 1, lines 72-94)?

1 Write about:

   a   the literal meanings of words
   b   their connotations
   c   the Prince's use of imagery and poetry
   d   how effective you find his persuasive techniques
   e   how successfully you think he asserts his power and authority.

2 Use examples from the text to support your ideas. You should also use the annotations from the sample responses to guide you in practising these skills.

GETTING FURTHER

Fate, the idea that our lives are shaped by forces beyond our control, is an important theme in *Romeo and Juliet*. How has reading and watching the first five scenes of the play developed your understanding of this theme? You might want to fill in a table like this one, to organise your thoughts.

What did I know when I read the Prologue?	Romeo and Juliet are 'star-crossed'.
What did I think then?	Fate has decided they will meet.
What do I know now, at the end of Scene 5?	Romeo already feels 'Some consequence yet hanging in the stars'.
What do I think now?	By agreeing to go to the party he is accepting his fate.

2

Act 2: Making the match

How does Shakespeare develop the play in Act 2?

Your progress in this unit:
- get an overview of the plot of Act 2
- understand how Shakespeare uses character, ideas and language
- think about ways in which the action may be presented in performance
- develop your written response skills.

GETTING STARTED – THE PLAY AND YOU

Thinking about Act 2

This act focuses on what happens after the Capulets' party, at which Romeo and Juliet met and fell in love.

Write a diary entry for the day after you have had an exciting, life-changing event. Concentrate on the wide range of emotions you might be experiencing (some joyful, some confusing?) and consider how your life can never be the same again.

GETTING CLOSER – FOCUS ON DETAILS

How does Shakespeare develop the plot in Act 2?

This unit covers the Chorus and the six scenes of Act 2. Read through the plot summary for each scene, to get an overview of Act 2.

Exploring the Chorus and Act 2 Scene 1

As in the Prologue that opened the play, Shakespeare uses the Chorus to open Act 2, this time to sum up what has taken place.

1 You are a scriptwriter who has been commissioned to rewrite the Chorus in modern **prose**. Write no more than five sentences, beginning:

'Now, as Romeo's old love for Rosaline is about to wither and die, his new love for Juliet blossoms ready to take its place … '

In Scene 1, with Romeo out of sight, Benvolio and Mercutio discuss where he has gone. Their contrasting suggestions provide further evidence of the differences in their characters. Mercutio believes initially that Romeo **'hath stol'n him home to bed'**. He claims that Romeo is **'humours! [a moody lover] madman! passion!'**. Benvolio, on the other hand, insists that Romeo **'ran this way and leapt this orchard wall.'** He assures Mercutio: **'Come, he hath hid himself among these trees'**.

2 In pairs, copy this table and complete it with phrases about Mercutio and Benvolio's attitudes. Try to link your answers to the text.

Attitude to:	Mercutio	Benvolio
Life		
Love	Full of mockery. Does not take it seriously.	
Friendship		Shows concern for Romeo.
Women		
Your suggestions		

The Chorus
The Chorus sums up what has happened to Romeo and Juliet, and the problems they face.

Scene 1
It is near dawn, Romeo arrives alone and hides near the wall of the Capulets' orchard. Benvolio and Mercutio arrive. He hears their conversation. Mercutio jokes about Romeo being dead; Benvolio suggests that he is simply hidden among the trees. Both think he is still depressed about Rosaline.

Scene 2
Romeo sees Juliet come to her window and he makes a speech about her beauty: '**The brightness of her cheek would shame those stars, / As daylight doth a lamp**'. He overhears her describing her love for him and her concern because he is a Montague. Romeo reveals himself and Juliet expresses her fear for his safety. Romeo asserts that his love is greater than his fear of death. Juliet is embarrassed, realising he has overheard her declaration of love. Romeo assures her of his devotion. The Nurse calls Juliet, and the lovers part.

Scene 3
Friar Lawrence is alone at daybreak, gathering herbs; he speaks of their medicinal and poisonous properties. Romeo arrives and tells of his love for Juliet. The Friar remarks on how easily young men's emotions change. Romeo explains his plan to marry Juliet in secret. The Friar agrees to help, hoping the match will heal the division between their families.

Scene 4
Benvolio and Mercutio meet. Mercutio speaks mockingly of Tybalt. Romeo arrives and has some youthful banter with Mercutio. The Nurse arrives and Mercutio makes fun of her. Benvolio and Mercutio leave. The Nurse asks Romeo what his intentions are towards Juliet. Romeo reveals his plan to marry her in secret and the Nurse agrees to help.

Scene 5
Juliet praises Romeo's good looks to the Nurse and reveals the planned secret marriage.

Scene 6
Romeo returns to Friar Lawrence and speaks boldly of his love. Friar Lawrence warns that '**violent delights have violent ends**'. Juliet arrives. She says she cannot fully express her joy. They go to be married.

> # But soft, what light through yonder window breaks? It is the east, and Juliet is the sun.
>
> *Romeo: Act 2 Scene 2, lines 2-3*

ACT 2 SCENE 2: 'THE BALCONY SCENE'

Setting and staging in Act 2 Scene 2

Act 2 Scene 2 is often called 'the balcony scene', although there is no actual balcony. Shakespeare's stage directions say nothing about the setting but modern editors often add some information to help you picture the scene. Shakespeare's **dialogue** in Act 2 Scenes 2 and 3 gives us five facts about what is happening, when and where:

- it is night
- they are in an orchard
- there is a wall
- there are trees
- Juliet is at the window.

1 Theatre companies often have very little money to spend. Describe the simplest scenery that you would need to stage this scene.

Character through language and imagery

Before Romeo makes himself known to Juliet, the audience hears each of them speaking separately. Romeo shows what he thinks of Juliet in lines 2–32. He begins:

> But soft, what light through yonder window breaks?
> It is the east, and Juliet is the sun.
> Arise, fair sun, and kill the envious moon,
> Who is already sick and pale with grief
> That thou, her maid, art far more fair than she.

1 By using **imagery** connected with light and brightness, he gives away his feelings. How many such references can you spot in his opening lines?

a   Trace how he uses these images through the rest of his speech.
b   Notice how many times he refers to Juliet's appearance and to '**eyes**'. What is the effect of these references?

> ### Contexts
>
> In Verona there is a balcony where Juliet is supposed to have stood, even though there is no balcony in the play and there was probably no historical Juliet to appear on it. That doesn't stop tourists visiting it, though.

Read more about language in *Romeo and Juliet* in Unit 10.

Now turn to Juliet's lines 33-49. Juliet begins:

O Romeo, Romeo, wherefore art thou Romeo?
Deny thy father and refuse thy name;
Or if thou wilt not, be but sworn my love,
And I'll no longer be a Capulet.

When Juliet later declares '**That which we call a rose / By any other word would smell as sweet**', she is saying that objects themselves (in this case, a rose) are more important than the names we give them.

2 What is the effect of Juliet repeating the word '**name**' so many times in these lines?

3 Copy lines 33-36 and 37-49. Then, using different-coloured pens, underline some examples of:

  a   repetition of words or phrases
  b   repetition of ideas
  c   lists
  d   questions and exclamations.

4 What is Juliet's overwhelming emotion in this passage?

5 What difference does the fact that she thinks she is alone make to the way you interpret her speech?

Contexts

In the opening of this scene (lines 1-9), Romeo refers to Juliet as '**the sun**', begging her to rise and '**kill the envious moon**'. His description of the moon as '**sick and green**' refers not only to the idea of envy but to the belief that girls who remained unmarried would become ill. Romeo also refers to the moon's '**vestal livery**' because the ancient Roman moon goddess Diana was the goddess of virginity. A 'vestal virgin' was a kind of nun, dedicated to the worship of Diana. These nuns remained virgins all their lives.

6 Now turn to the part of the scene where Juliet discovers she is not alone.

  a   What is Juliet's first concern when she discovers that Romeo is present (lines 49-63)?
  b   What is her dominant emotion in her next speeches (lines 62-65, 70, 74)?

7 The 'balcony scene' is a very important point in the play. By the time it ends, Romeo and Juliet have promised to marry each other.

  a   Work in pairs to pick out the ten most important moments or episodes in Act 2 Scene 2. Make sure that each 'moment' is clearly linked to an extract from the text.
  b   You could then go on to produce a storyboard that illustrates your choices. Display this for comparison with storyboards from other pairs.

What's in a name? That which we call a rose
By any other word would smell as sweet

Juliet: Act 2 Scene 2, lines 43-44

Fain would I dwell on form, fain, fain deny
What I have spoke

Juliet: Act 2 Scene 2, lines 88-89

 Learning checkpoint

During lines 85–127, Juliet wishes she had had the chance to respond to Romeo's speech properly. She also worries that Romeo may lose respect for her, or that his own feelings may not be sincere.

Q Below are three quotations from this passage:

a 'Fain would I dwell on form, fain, fain deny / What I have spoke'
b ' … thou mayst think my behaviour light'
c 'What satisfaction canst thou have tonight?'

Look at this interpretation of of **quotation a** below. Then write a paragraph exploring **quotations b** and **c**, showing what Juliet is thinking and feeling.

Juliet is confused and anxious that what she has said to Romeo may lead to his losing respect for her. Possibly it would be better for her to 'deny / What I have spoke'. Juliet insists that she would gladly stick to speaking and behaving with ceremony and politeness. This is the way she usually behaves (perhaps the way she has been brought up?). But directly after this quotation she rejects 'form' as something that may be false and contrived. As she speaks about love to Romeo, she wants to express herself with truth, simplicity and integrity.

This may mark a turning point in the presentation of Juliet as she begins to appreciate that simple, direct language is the only way to express her intimate feelings. This is very different from the polite and restrained Juliet we saw on her first appearance in Act 1.

How will I know I've done this well?

✔ The **best answers** will explore Shakespeare's presentation of the character of Juliet. They will offer a personal response and provide many, carefully analysed details based on the language of the play.
✔ **Good answers** will show a clear understanding of Juliet's presentation but with fewer analytical details.
✔ **Weaker answers** will only explain Juliet's presentation in a general sense and will use limited evidence from the text.

 Now watch a video about the 'balcony scene' on Cambridge Elevate.

ACT 2 SCENES 3 AND 4: THE FRIAR, MERCUTIO AND THE NURSE

Performing Romeo's meeting with the Friar, Act 2 Scene 3

 In most copies of the play, Romeo enters Act 2 Scene 3 at line 23, and does not greet the Friar until line 31. The Friar seems to be lost in a world of his own ('**What early tongue so sweet saluteth me?**', and Romeo is reluctant to disturb him.

a   What do you think is the reason for Romeo's reluctance?

b   With a classmate, discuss what you think Romeo's attitude is at the beginning of this scene, and experiment with ways of performing the opening to show this.

Use of language, form and structure

Shakespeare often uses a rhyming **couplet** at the end of a major speech or a scene to indicate that the speaker has arrived at an important decision or that a debate is now concluded.

 All Friar Lawrence's speeches in this scene are written in rhyming couplets. Do you think this approach makes the Friar seem:

a   clever but superficial

b   old, wise and dignified?

> **Read more about language in *Romeo and Juliet* in Unit 10.**

 When Romeo begins speaking, he adopts the pattern of the Friar's language, so that the entire scene is rhymed, with one character completing a rhyme started by the other, as their dialogue progresses.

- Try to come up with one reason why Shakespeare might have chosen to do this.
- Work in pairs. Discuss whether the scene would work better if it were performed with the actors clearly emphasising all the rhymes or whether this would make it too predictable and boring.
- The dialogue explores contrasts between Romeo and the Friar in a number of key areas. Copy and complete this table.

Romeo's naivety	
Romeo's youthfulness	
Romeo's haste	
Friar Lawrence's wisdom	
Friar Lawrence's age	
Friar Lawrence's caution	

> 🔑 **Key terms**
>
> **couplet:** a unit of two lines of poetry, often used in 'rhyming couplet'.

What early tongue so sweet saluteth me?

Friar Lawrence: Act 2 Scene 3, line 32

For nought so vile, that on the earth doth live, But to the earth some special good doth give

Friar Lawrence: Act 2 Scene 3, lines 17-18

Developing ideas and perspectives

Near the opening of this scene as he gathers herbs, the Friar speaks of the '**powerful grace**' which is in all things.

> For nought so vile, that on the earth doth live,
> But to the earth some special good doth give;
> Nor ought so good but, strained from that fair use,
> Revolts from true birth, stumbling on abuse.

Friar Lawrence: Act 2 Scene 3, lines 17-20

In lines 27-30, he goes on to say how this is true of men - that '**grace**' and '**rude will**' exist in all people, and their fate is determined by which of these qualities plays a greater part in their actions. Through the Friar's words, Shakespeare offers the audience a perspective from which to judge the character and actions of the major figures in the play.

1 Working in pairs or small groups, discuss and examine the **connotations** of the words '**grace**' and '**rude will**'. What do these terms mean to you? And what do you think they would have meant to Shakespeare's audience?

2 Based on your reading of the play so far, assess each of the major characters you have encountered, from this perspective. This spider diagram shows one example.

Read more about ideas in *Romeo and Juliet* in Unit 9.

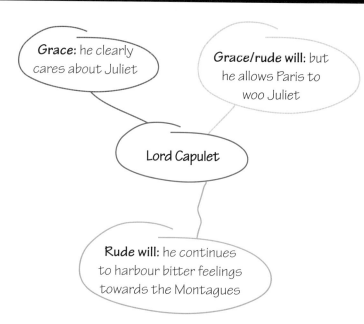

- **Grace:** he clearly cares about Juliet
- **Grace/rude will:** but he allows Paris to woo Juliet
- Lord Capulet
- **Rude will:** he continues to harbour bitter feelings towards the Montagues

3 How would you assess the Friar's actions in this scene? Draw your own flow chart showing his actions from the perspective of '**grace**' versus '**rude will**'.

Mercutio's character in Act 2 Scene 4

The teenage humour the audience has come to expect from Mercutio dominates the first 120 lines of Scene 4. He makes sexually suggestive jokes, sings rude **verse**, and targets various characters with his mockery: '**this drivelling love is like a great natural that runs lolling up and down to hide his bauble in a hole**'. He starts by continuing the **theme** of his joke from Scene 1, pretending to mourn for Romeo. Then he shifts to a scathing description of Tybalt, mocking his swordsmanship. Finally he makes some very unkind jokes at the Nurse's expense.

1 Explore the motivation behind Mercutio's mockery.

a   In groups of 4–5, prepare a hot-seating exercise in which Mercutio is questioned by other characters. Use the discussion points in the box to help you choose who should interrogate him.

b   After the questioning, each group should consider whether there is any evidence in the text to support Mercutio's answers.

Ideas, attitudes and perspectives

In this scene Shakespeare presents the Nurse from two very different perspectives. To begin with, the young men's attitude to her makes her seem like a figure of fun (lines 83–120). After Benvolio and Mercutio leave, the dialogue between Romeo and the Nurse continues in prose until Romeo reveals his plan to marry Juliet and enlists her help.

1 How and why does our perception of the Nurse change when Romeo's friends leave?

2 The figure of the Nurse has divided critics and audiences over the years. What do you think Shakespeare's attitude is to the character of the Nurse? Respond to the statements in this table and add two additional ones.

> **Discussion points for Mercutio**
>
> - Does the fact that Mercutio continues to make negative comments about Romeo's love life suggest that it's an issue that bothers him more than he can admit?
> - Is his mockery of Tybalt simply due to the fact that Tybalt is a Capulet?
> - Why does he pick on Tybalt's swordsmanship?
> - What does his treatment of the Nurse add to your impression of his attitude to women?
> - What does it show about his attitude to the older generation?

The significance of the Nurse

Interpretation	Strongly agree	Agree	Disagree	Strongly disagree
She is only of importance for her comic value.				
She is mainly of importance for her comic value, but also plays a major role in developing the plot.				
She is more important as an older and more experienced figure who represents the world of adult values in the play.				
As Juliet's confidante, she genuinely cares about her and has Juliet's interests at heart throughout.				
Her compassion, understanding and insight make her a very sympathetic character.				

Now turn this table into a paragraph of writing, putting forward your interpretation and including evidence from the text to support it.

… this drivelling love is like a great natural that runs lolling up and down to hide his bauble in a hole.

Mercutio: Act 2 Scene 4, lines 74–75

ACT 2 SCENES 5 AND 6: CONTEXT AND LANGUAGE

The Nurse in context in Act 2 Scene 5

1 As her one-time wet nurse, the Nurse's relationship with Juliet is clearly a close one. If you were directing a production set in today's society, would you present the Nurse as Juliet's:

a child-minder
b nanny
c former primary-school teacher
d aunt or a friend of the family?

2 In lines 38–43, the Nurse praises Romeo. Write out these lines and highlight references to his body and his personality.

a What does the nature of her praise add to your interpretation of her character?
b What other evidence can you find in the scene to support this view?

'I pray thee'

1 Juliet is impatient, but also seems sympathetic towards the Nurse.

a Working with a classmate, discuss how you would direct the actress playing Juliet so that her actions show the character's mixed emotions.
b Use this example and add some more of your own.

Juliet's language	Director's notes advising Juliet how to move, and how to use gesture, tone and pitch to signal her impatience
Her **soliloquy** (lines 1–17), waiting impatiently for the Nurse: 'The clock struck nine when I did send the Nurse; / In half an hour she promised to return.'	Juliet paces anxiously around her bedroom. She sighs before line 1, emphasises the word 'nine' and stamps her feet at the end of line 2 …
Greeting the Nurse's arrival (lines 21–24): 'O Lord, why look'st thou sad?'	
Urging the Nurse to speak (lines 27–28; 31–37): 'Nay, come, I pray thee speak, good, good Nurse, speak.'	
Your own examples	

c As an extension activity, complete a similar table for the Nurse's speeches in this scene. Then consider why she seems to drag out her replies to Juliet so much when Juliet is so desperate to hear her news about Romeo.

Read more about the context of *Romeo and Juliet* in Unit 7.

Contexts

In the 16th century, rich women who did not want to breastfeed employed wet nurses (new mothers with breast milk). The Nurse was employed by Lady Capulet shortly after the birth of the Nurse's own child, Susan, who then died (Act 1 Scene 3, lines 19–21). Long after her role as wet nurse ceased, the Nurse was kept on by the Capulets to care for their only child.

Key terms

soliloquy: a long speech given by a character, usually alone on stage, as if they are thinking aloud.

The context of Act 2 Scene 6

1 Read the following list of statements. Then decide which ones you think would have been normal for Shakespeare's audience, and which ones they would have found unusual or unacceptable:

a   Two children from wealthy families marry.
b   Two children from wealthy families marry without a long engagement.
c   Two children from wealthy families marry without their parents' consent.
d   Two children from wealthy families marry for love.
e   Two children from wealthy families are married by a Catholic friar.

2 Based on your responses, describe the impact that you think this scene might have had on Shakespeare's audience.

3 Does it have a similar impact on you? Explain your answer.

Character through language and imagery

Romeo makes bold statements of his love and his determination to defy all danger but the Friar warns against hasty behaviour. He uses powerful imagery in his description of Romeo and Juliet's love (lines 9–15). Working with a classmate, copy the table below and fill in the gaps to build on the explanation of the Friar's language.

SKILL	'violent delights'	which in their 'triumph die'	like 'fire and powder'	which as they 'kiss consume'
explain	powerful gestures of love	which don't last, but end as soon as they are expressed	are like fire and gunpowder	which blaze fiercely and are gone in the moment they meet
examine	'violence' connotes conflict and aggression which contradicts the idea of delight which suggests pleasure	'triumph' has connotations of _____ 'die' suggests _____	'fire' and 'powder' have connotations of _____	'kiss' but 'consume'
analyse	This suggests that hot-headed young lovers delight in _____ This links to the Prologue's themes of _____			

These violent delights have violent ends,
And in their triumph die like fire and powder ...

Friar Lawrence: Act 2 Scene 6, lines 9–10

They are but beggars that can count their worth,
But my true love is grown to such excess
I cannot sum up sum of half my wealth.

Juliet: Act 2 Scene 6, lines 32–34

Ask Juliet

Juliet arrives, the Friar greets her and Juliet expresses her joy at being in love: ' **… my true love is grown to such excess / I cannot sum up sum of half my wealth.**' Almost immediately the Friar offers to marry her to Romeo: '**you shall not stay alone / Till Holy Church incorporate two in one.**' By the time we next see Juliet in Act 3, she is married. This is a huge step for a thirteen-year-old girl to take so quickly, especially as she is acting directly against her parents' wishes.

1 Write three questions that you would like to ask Juliet at this point. Make sure that they are clearly connected with what has happened to her so far in the play. Take the opportunity to explore her feelings, her motivation for her actions and her relationships with other characters. Use the text as the starting point to generate your questions.

GETTING IT INTO WRITING

You have looked at how Shakespeare explores differences in attitudes of the young and the old throughout Act 2. For example Scene 3 ends with Romeo urging: '**O let us hence, I stand on sudden haste**'. Friar Lawrence, in contrast, advises: '**Wisely and slow, they stumble that run fast**'. Juliet, in Scene 5, observes: '**Love's heralds should be thoughts, / Which ten times faster glides than the sun's beams**'. The Nurse implores: '**Jesu, what haste! can you not stay a while?**'

In this section you will produce a detailed essay plan for one of the two following questions:

How does Shakespeare present the attitude of the young towards the old in Act 2?

What is Shakespeare suggesting about the effect of love on the behaviour of the young in Act 2?

Complete this assignment on Cambridge Elevate.

In pairs, choose your question. Then, on your own, plan your answer. Look quickly back through Act 2 and gather key quotations and ideas. Compare your planning notes with your partner and together decide on which ideas and references are the strongest ones. Help each other to produce an essay plan. Once you are happy with your plan, you are ready to write your essay:

- Arrange your plan and notes from the unit in front of you, and start writing.
- Check your work when you have finished.
- Compare finished essays with your partner and learn from anything you think they are doing better than you.

 Learning checkpoint

How will I know I've done this well?

✔ **The best answers** will offer well-written interpretations of the evidence in specific scenes, commenting on how Shakespeare explores key issues and considering their impact. Quotations will be embedded in the writing and skilfully analysed.

✔ **Good answers** will show a clear understanding of how Shakespeare dramatises the issues, using well-chosen examples from a number of scenes in Act 2. They may comment on specific words or phrases used in the text. They will use accurate spelling and clear sentences.

✔ **Weaker answers** will comment on the question in general, using few or no specific examples and not mentioning why Shakespeare might use them or how they might affect the audience.

GETTING FURTHER

1 Critics often talk about major characters and minor characters. In addition to Romeo and Juliet, which other characters would you call 'major' on the basis of Acts 1 and 2? What evidence in the text leads you to this opinion?

List of possible characters:

- Benvolio
- Mercutio
- Tybalt
- Paris
- The Prince
- Lord Capulet
- Lady Capulet
- Lord Montague
- The Nurse
- Friar Lawrence

2 Several of Shakespeare's plays deal with relationships between fathers and daughters and the painful consequences of going against parents' wishes.

a Find a copy of *The Merchant of Venice* and look at what happens to the relationship between Shylock and his daughter Jessica when she rejects him and his Jewish religion and runs away to marry a Christian.

b You could also watch the film *Twilight* (2008) or read Ian McEwan's novel *Atonement* to see how these works explore the theme of love developing in difficult circumstances.

For by your leaves, you shall not stay alone
Till Holy Church incorporate two in one.

Friar Lawrence: Act 2 Scene 6, lines 36–37

3

Act 3: Murder and separation

How does the plot develop in Act 3?

Your progress in this unit:
- explore how Shakespeare develops plot, character and ideas
- analyse Shakespeare's use of language, imagery, form and structure
- explore ways in which the action may be presented in performance
- develop a response to a writing task.

GETTING STARTED - THE PLAY AND YOU

Thinking about Act 3

Act 3 centres on a key incident – Romeo's revenge against Tybalt for the murder of Mercutio, and Romeo's later punishment by being banished (made to leave his homeland). This forces the lovers to consider that they may never be together again.

1 Imagine you are separated from a friend or loved one. Write a letter to this person expressing your feelings about the situation.

GETTING CLOSER - FOCUS ON DETAILS

Plot development

This unit covers the five scenes of Act 3. Read through the key details for each scene, to get an overview of Act 3.

Each of the following quotations is taken from one of the five scenes in Act 3.

Capulet: Hang thee, young baggage, disobedient wretch!
I tell thee what: get thee to church a'Thursday,
Or never after look me in the face.

Juliet: Come, gentle Night, come, loving, black-browed Night,
Give me my Romeo …

Capulet: Go you to Juliet ere you go to bed,
Prepare her, wife, against this wedding day.

Friar Lawrence: Here from Verona art thou banishèd.
Be patient, for the world is broad and wide.

Tybalt: Romeo, the love I bear thee can afford
No better term than this: thou art a villain.

1 Use the summary of the scenes to help you place the quotations in the correct order.

2 Explain what each quotation tells you about what happens in Act 3.

Scene 1
Mercutio and Benvolio meet Tybalt in the street. Tybalt accuses Mercutio of associating with Romeo and they square up to each other. Romeo enters and tries to stop the fight but will not get involved. This angers Mercutio, who is wounded while fighting Tybalt and later dies of his wounds. Romeo is furious; he kills Tybalt and runs away. The Prince arrives and declares that Romeo will be banished from Verona for ever.

Scene 2
Juliet is alone in her room, longing for night and Romeo's return. The Nurse arrives in a state of shock, and reveals that Romeo has been banished. Juliet feels torn between grief for her murdered cousin Tybalt and her love for Romeo. The Nurse promises to bring Romeo to her bedchamber. Juliet gives her a ring to take to him.

Scene 3
This scene is set in Friar Lawrence's cell (room), where Romeo learns of his banishment. The Friar tries to comfort Romeo. The Nurse arrives, sees Romeo weeping, and criticises him for his weakness. Romeo speaks of killing himself, and the Friar rebukes him angrily. Then the Friar suggests a plan to enable the lovers to be together again.

Scene 4
Lord Capulet, his wife and Paris meet at the Capulets' house. Capulet promises Paris that he will get Juliet to agree to their marriage by Thursday. In view of Tybalt's death, Capulet suggests that the ceremony will be small. Capulet sends his wife to inform Juliet of the arrangement.

Scene 5
This scene takes place at daybreak, at Juliet's window. The lovers sorrowfully say farewell. Juliet expresses her fear that she will never see Romeo again. Lady Capulet arrives and mistakenly believes that Juliet is mourning Tybalt. She attempts to cheer her daughter up by telling her that her marriage to Paris is planned for Thursday. Lord Capulet arrives and is enraged when Juliet refuses to marry Paris. He threatens to disown her. The Nurse advises Juliet to forget Romeo and accept Paris. The Nurse leaves and Juliet vows to refuse her advice and goes instead to visit Friar Lawrence.

1: TWO MURDERS

and theatricality

Scene 1 is often referred to as 'the fight scene'. It brings to life a key element of the play – the conflict between youthful, aggressive, male pride and mature reason. Tybalt and Mercutio represent youthful aggression, while Benvolio is the voice of reason. Romeo is caught between the two. His love for Juliet represents a step towards responsible maturity, but this is counteracted by his continuing loyalty to his youthful friends and relatives – particularly Mercutio.

1 Working in a small group, read through lines 33–48. Then improvise action shots (as if you were making a film) for each of the exchanges between:

a Mercutio and Tybalt (lines 33–35, 36–38, 39–42)
b Benvolio and Mercutio (43–48)
c Romeo and Tybalt (lines 53–65).

2 One group member can direct, making suggestions about movements, gestures and ways of speaking.

a Rehearse these exchanges and then film them or perform them to the class.
b Ask for feedback on how effectively you have shown the characters' thoughts and feelings.

Exploring the meaning of language

Between Mercutio's wounding and Benvolio's announcement that he is dead, Romeo questions the effect his love for Juliet has had on him.

1 Read lines 100–106 closely and discuss their meaning in a group.

2 Romeo calls himself '**effeminate**', commenting that Juliet has changed him. Make a copy of this spidergram and use it to list some of the qualities you would expect a more '**effeminate**' Romeo to show. The word bank contains some suggestions for you to consider.

3 How would Romeo react to these qualities in himself, and how would Juliet react to them?

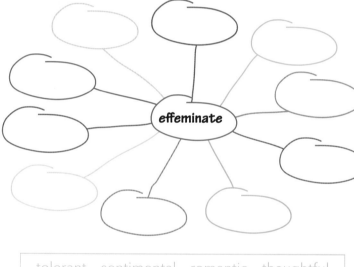

effeminate

tolerant   sentimental   romantic   thoughtful

O sweet Juliet,
Thy beauty hath made me effeminate,
And in my temper softened valour's steel!

Romeo: Act 3 Scene 1, lines 104–106

4 Romeo uses the word '**steel**' to indicate masculine qualities that have been '**softened**' by the influence of his love for Juliet. Create a second diagram exploring the connotations of this word. Again, the word bank contains some suggestions for you to consider.

a Discuss the connotations you have suggested. Which do you think Romeo considers important? Which would Juliet object to?

b What image of masculinity is Shakespeare creating with these contrasting qualities and connotations?

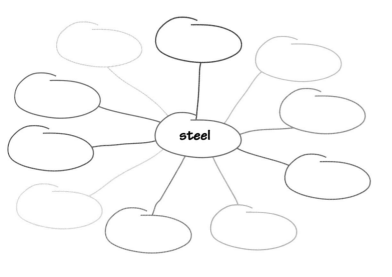

cold   hard   determination

Ideas and different perspectives

Away to heaven, respective lenity,
And fire-eyed fury be my conduct now!

Romeo: Act 3 Scene 1, lines 114–115

 Read more about ideas in *Romeo and Juliet* in Unit 9.

1 This diagram represents the moment at which Romeo must decide whether to avenge Mercutio's death or turn away. Copy the two bubbles onto a large sheet of paper. In your group, discuss the thoughts in Romeo's mind that urge him to take revenge on Tybalt. Write these in the red bubble. Discuss the thoughts urging him to turn away, and write these in the blue bubble. Then answer the following questions:

a Why do you think he gives in to the urge to take revenge?

b Is he right to do so? Explain your answer.

2 Having killed Tybalt, Romeo realises the implications of what he has done. He describes himself as '**fortune's fool**'.

a What does Romeo mean by this phrase?

b How does it develop the idea of fate that was introduced in the Prologue?

c Why do you think the Prince decides against sentencing Romeo to death?

 Explore the scene where Mercutio is stabbed on Cambridge Elevate.

Gallop apace, you fiery-footed steeds,
Towards Phoebus' lodging

Juliet: Act 3 Scene 2, lines 1–2

ACT 3 SCENE 2: EXPLORING JULIET'S RESPONSE TO NEWS OF ROMEO

Juliet's opening speech: language and imagery

1 Read Juliet's opening speech (lines 1–31) and decide which words you think best describe Juliet's emotional state at this point: impatient, calm, resigned, excited.

2 Juliet's speech shows how marriage to Romeo has changed her.

  a How has her language changed since her meeting with Romeo at the window of her chamber? Is she still practical and cautious in the way she speaks?

  b How does Shakespeare use Juliet's speech to foreshadow the idea of disaster?

  c Use this table to explore her imagery.

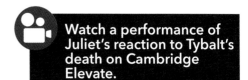

Watch a performance of Juliet's reaction to Tybalt's death on Cambridge Elevate.

Read lines	Contextual information	Discussion
1–4	'Gallop apace, you fiery-footed steeds' In Greek myth Phaeton, the child of the Sun, took the reins of his father's chariot. The horses galloped away, bringing night early, and bringing disaster to the world.	**Explain:** why Juliet longs for night to come early. **Explore:** how the connotations of the words and this image affect your interpretation of Juliet's statement.
10–13	'Thou sober-suited matron all in black' The matron (an older woman) is a poetic device, a personification of night. She is being asked for advice about a first sexual experience.	**Explain:** what Juliet wants the night to teach her. **Explore:** the connotations of the image and words such as 'civil', 'Night', 'sober', 'matron', 'all in black'.
17–19	'For thou wilt lie upon the wings of night' In Greek myths the raven is associated with good luck, but in British myths it is linked with death. New snow symbolises purity and beauty, but also suggests the coming of winter.	**Explain:** how Juliet describes Romeo's beauty. **Explore:** the conflict between the positive and negative connotations of the raven and the snow; and what they add to your interpretation of Juliet's words.

 Read more about language in *Romeo and Juliet* in Unit 10.

Juliet and the Nurse: characterisation and ideas

1 In lines 35–70, the Nurse confuses Juliet into thinking Romeo is dead: '**Alack the day, he's gone, he's killed, he's dead!**' Having finally understood that in fact Romeo has killed Tybalt, Juliet questions her belief in Romeo's good qualities.

a Copy out Juliet's reaction to this news in lines 73–79.

b Highlight all the examples of **antithesis** she uses (for example '**Beautiful tyrant**').

c How does her language represent her emotional conflict?

2 Lines 105–126 show Juliet's response to Romeo's banishment.

a What do you think Juliet is saying? Is she relieved or despairing?

b Working in small groups, focus on lines 114–120 and discuss the following interpretations:
  • losing Tybalt and her parents would be easier to cope with than Romeo's banishment
  • the death of her parents would be preferable to Romeo's banishment
  • Romeo's banishment is like her own death and the death of everyone she cares for.

c Which interpretation is best supported by the text?

3 Read and discuss lines 85–89.

a What view of men does the Nurse express in these lines?

b Do you think she is sincere? Or is she simply saying what she thinks Juliet wants to hear?

c What quality of the Nurse's character does this suggest to you? Consider for example: loyalty, weakness, bitterness.

4 Look at the way Juliet reacts at lines 43 and 90.

a Is she fair in her treatment of the Nurse?

b Is Juliet's attitude understandable?

5 This word bank contains words and phrases describing Juliet's emotions during this scene.

a Write them out in order, to indicate how Juliet's emotions change as the scene progresses. Add additional phrases of your own where necessary.

b Find a quotation from the text to support each word or phrase.

| anger at the Nurse   hatred of Romeo   guilt |
| longing   relief   shock   grief   despair |

Key terms

poetic device: a technique used by a poet, such as personification.
personification: the poetic device of giving human qualities to an object.
foreshadow: hint at what lies ahead.
antithesis: two opposite ideas that are put together to achieve a contrasting effect.
myth: an ancient, traditional story, often about early history and sometimes involving magic.

ACT 3 SCENE 3: ROMEO'S BANISHMENT

Contexts

Having been sentenced to banishment by the Prince, Romeo is now an outcast: '**There is no world without Verona walls**'. In Shakespeare's time, a sentence of banishment was rare; yet his plays contain several examples of people who are forced to leave their own countries and live abroad. Perhaps this reflects his own experience of leaving his home and family in Stratford and moving to London.

Romeo and the Friar

1 Read lines 1–70.

a   Which of the two characters, Romeo or the Friar, do you think is more in control in this passage? Relate your answer to evidence in the text.

b   Select the words that you think best describe Romeo's attitude in the passage:

sad	angry	despondent
self-pitying	ungrateful	petulant

c   Find evidence from the text to support your choice.

2 How does Romeo's attitude to the Friar in this scene resemble Juliet's attitude to the Nurse in Act 3 Scene 2? Describe the similarities you notice in their attitudes.

3 This word bank contains words describing the Friar's attitude to Romeo during this scene.

anger	sympathy	exasperation	patience

a   Draw a flow diagram with at least four boxes and arrows and write in the words, to indicate the development of the Friar's mood as the scene progresses. Add additional words of your own where you feel they are necessary.

b   Find an extract from the text to illustrate each description of the Friar's mood.

Storyboarding Romeo and the Friar's relationship in this scene

Create four single frames illustrating the action between Romeo and Friar Lawrence. Each frame must have a narrative strip, at least one speech bubble, at least one thought bubble, and a sketch of the two characters (stick figures will do). Use arrows to indicate the position of each character in relation to the other, and their gestures.

Arrange your frames in order to create a storyboard and discuss how the relationship between the two characters develops throughout the scene.

There is no world without Verona walls,
But purgatory, torture, hell itself

Romeo: Act 3 Scene 3, lines 17–18

Romeo's language in Act 3 Scene 3

 Copy out lines 29–51 and highlight examples of Romeo referring to himself in the third person (as 'Romeo' rather than 'I' or 'me').

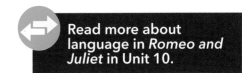
Read more about language in *Romeo and Juliet* in Unit 10.

a   Why do you think Romeo is doing this?

b   Rewrite his speech, replacing the word 'Romeo' with 'I' or 'me' as appropriate.

c   Read both versions aloud. How does the impact of the changed version differ from the original?

d   Do you think Romeo speaks this way because:
   • it is easier to deal with his pain if he pretends it has happened to someone else?
   • he is in shock and feels disconnected from himself?
   • he is banished, and feels like an outcast from his old life and identity?
   • he is deliberately torturing himself by speaking as if he is his own punisher?

   Explain your choice.

Learning checkpoint

The drama of this whole act centres on Romeo's banishment, so make sure that you can explain:

✔ how this key event happened

✔ why it happened

✔ its significance to the play as a whole.

Q   Write an account of Romeo's banishment and its consequences.

You should:

a   describe the characters who played a role in this incident and explain the part they played in it

b   analyse Romeo's choices and motives, supporting your interpretation with evidence from the text

c   discuss the themes Shakespeare is encouraging us to think about during and after this event. Here are some possibilities to start you off: thought and emotion; youth and age; love and loyalty; personal choices and fate.

How will I know I've done this well?

✔ The **best answers** will suggest and discuss interpretations based on analysis of action and language.

✔ **Good answers** will give an interpretation of action supported by textual evidence.

✔ **Weaker answers** will simply explain the action, using evidence from the text.

ACT 3 SCENES 4 AND 5: AUTHORITY AND DISOBEDIENCE

The context of Scene 4

1 How would a modern Western audience react to this scene? Discuss the reasons for this reaction.

2 If you were in Juliet's situation, would you:

- accept the arrangement without argument
- resent the decision but co-operate with it
- refuse to co-operate?

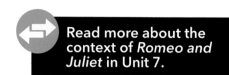

Read more about the context of *Romeo and Juliet* in Unit 7.

> **ℹ Contexts**
>
> Juliet's marriage to Paris would be an event of great significance to her and her family. Her father has arranged it, without much discussion with Juliet. This was common practice among wealthy Elizabethan families, and would have seemed perfectly normal to Shakespeare's audience.

Lord and Lady Capulet: attitudes and relationship

1 How would you describe Capulet's attitude in this scene? This word bank has some suggestions that you could use.

arrogant	ignorant	overbearing
practical	caring	responsible

Show evidence from the text to support your description.

There is little direct evidence of Lady Capulet's response to her husband in this scene.

2 How would you interpret Lady Capulet's attitude to her husband? Explain your answer by referring to what she says and does in earlier scenes.

3 As director, how would you convey your interpretation of Lord and Lady Capulet's relationship in this scene? Make director's notes referring to:

- gesture
- facial expression
- tone of voice.

Context and ideas in Scene 5

In this scene, Juliet openly defies her parents. This would have seemed more shocking to an Elizabethan audience than it does today, as children were expected to obey their parents' wishes at all times.

1 Think of a situation in which you have been disobedient. Draw on your experience to describe what you think Juliet must be going through.

2 a Compare what Juliet says in lines 60-64 with Romeo's declaration in Act 3 Scene 1 that he is '**Fortune's fool**'.

    b Juliet addresses Fortune directly. What is she asking Fortune to do?

    c How might a modern audience react differently to her plea than audiences in Shakespeare's time?

 Explore the first part of Act 3 Scene 5 on Cambridge Elevate.

Juliet and her parents

 Explore the part of this scene where Juliet argues with her father on Cambridge Elevate.

1 Find evidence in the text that Lady Capulet:

    a does not believe in the strength of Juliet's feelings

    b has no idea of Juliet's true needs

    c is capable of ruthless actions.

2 What evidence can you find in this scene that the Nurse feels more loyalty and tenderness towards Juliet than her mother does?

3 Describe Juliet's attitude. Justify your description with evidence from the text. You could use the following quotations.

Juliet (lines 116–117): Now by Saint Peter's Church
    and Peter too,
He shall not make me there a joyful bride.

Juliet shows reckless defiance (and courage?) in swearing to her mother that she will not marry Paris.

Juliet (lines 158–159): Good father, I beseech you
    on my knees,
Hear me with patience but to speak a word.

Juliet displays humility in the face of her father's towering rage.

4 Find evidence in lines 176–195 for these statements about Lord Capulet:

    a He thinks Paris will be a good son-in-law.

    b He wants nobody in his family to go against his wishes.

    c He regards his daughter as a possession.

    d He believes that if he breaks a promise he loses his honour.

For each point, explain why you think it is important.

 Watch the video exploring the end of Act 3 Scene 7 on Cambridge Elevate.

 Contexts

In Shakespeare's time, it was believed that people had little ability to choose their own destiny. Instead, fate (or Fortune) was believed to control people's lives. Sometimes fate was linked to astrology, as when the Chorus describes Romeo and Juliet as '**star-cross'd lovers**'. The implication is that the couple could not avoid falling in love and dying because their fate had already been decided by the position of the stars when they were born.

GETTING IT INTO WRITING

One of the assessment objectives rewarded in your writing about literature is context. For drama, this includes the setting and use of the stage. Below is a question, followed by extracts from two responses in which the students have chosen to focus on this aspect of context.

How does Shakespeare present the attitudes of the young men in Act 3 Scene 1? Write about the language they use and the way their actions and performance might be staged.

a   the language they use
b   the way their actions and performance might be staged.

Complete this assignment on Cambridge Elevate.

RESPONSE 1

Benvolio is more mature than Mercutio. This shows when he says, 'The day is hot, the Capels are abroad, / And if we meet we shall not scape a brawl', because he knows they all feel tired and angry. This is not something you could easily show on stage, so it would be shown in the way they move or the tone of their voice. Mercutio comes across as arrogant in his speech. When Tybalt arrives, he seems up for a fight straight away because when Tybalt says he wants 'a word' Mercutio says he should add 'a blow'. This makes me imagine them like men outside a pub showing off to their mates by acting hard. But here it's not just fists but swords, so it's more dramatic for the audience, but not very realistic. Romeo starts off not wanting to fight Tybalt. This is because he is married to Juliet, so I don't think he should look or sound scared, but like he just doesn't want to fight. But when Mercutio is killed, he loses his temper. This would be shown from how loud he speaks and how crazy he is when he fights him.

> begins to explain

> some understanding of theatrical context

> begins to link performance context to question

> begins to use relevant subject terminology

> begins to understand ideas

RESPONSE 2

The conflict between adolescent ego and maturity is the key to this scene. Of course, pride and aggression are not limited to the young men. In Act 1 Scene 1, both Montague and Capulet are eager to get involved in the brawl – a sight intended to be theatrically comic, as is suggested by the fact that when Capulet calls for his sword, his wife responds 'A crutch, a crutch!'. In this scene, the confrontations and their consequences are more serious, and in the figure of Romeo the audience sees that key conflict personified. The immaturity of Mercutio and Tybalt, reaching immediately for their swords, is clear. One recalls Mercutio in Act 2 Scene 4, making fun of Tybalt's swordplay, possibly flourishing his own blade in mockery, 'he rests his minim rests, one, two and the third in your bosom … '. This later scene is an extension of this behaviour. For men like Mercutio, the sword is an extension of the ego. This was once the case for Romeo, but his sense of identity is no longer so clear to him. In media such as film, the conflict which rages inside Romeo between the desire for revenge and the knowledge of what he may be throwing away could be easily presented by voiceover, or flashback, but for Shakespeare, the emphasis must be on the way language

> clear understanding of implicit ideas

> specific link between performance context and question

> beginning to show thoughtful consideration of ideas and performance context

> thoughtful consideration of ideas

<u>directs the performance</u>. When Romeo reflects on his passivity, addressing the absent Juliet 'O Sweet … ' <u>one may imagine the tenderness of his voice</u>. Yet the following line 'Thy beauty has made me effeminate' suggests a hardening of tone, a note of self-disgust, emphasised further by the exclamation 'And in my temper softened valour's steel!'…

analyses theatrical effects of language

Learning checkpoint

Now write 300 words in answer to this question:

Q   How does Shakespeare use dialogue and action to present the character of Friar Lawrence in Act 3 Scene 3?

Use what you have studied in this unit to help you plan your answer. Write about how:

- the Friar's attitude to Romeo develops throughout the scene
- this is presented through their dialogue
- the dialogue might be supported by the staging of the scene.

How will I know I've done this well?

✔   Make clear links between theatrical context, the text and the question you are set
✔   Understand, explore and examine those links
✔   Understand, explore and examine ideas in the text, and their connection to the staging and performance
✔   Use examples from the text to support your ideas.

GETTING FURTHER

1   Use the internet to find the performances of the 'fight scene' (Act 3 Scene 1) in the 1968 Franco Zeffirelli film version of *Romeo and Juliet* and in the 1996 Baz Luhrmann film version.

   a   After watching each performance, write down at least two aspects of the direction or performance that you found effective.
   b   Working in pairs, compare your lists.
   c   Plan a performance of the fight using the best suggestions from your combined lists.

4

Act 4: A wedding and a funeral

How does Shakespeare move his characters from joy to grief in Act 4?

Your progress in this unit:

- explore the ways in which Shakespeare presents Juliet's feelings at this stage of the play
- analyse Shakespeare's use of language and imagery and its impact on the audience
- consider ways in which the action may be presented in performance
- select and use appropriate detail to write about the way Juliet's character is presented.

GETTING STARTED – THE PLAY AND YOU

1 Read these comments from members of an audience, saying how they feel about Juliet and her situation at the beginning of Act 4:

A 'I feel really sorry for her. She is desperately in love with Romeo but he let her down badly when he killed Tybalt. He has caused all her problems. I know she loved him but he has placed her in an impossible situation. He is so thoughtless; she is so vulnerable.'

B 'Her parents have treated her appallingly. They have made no attempt at all to find out what is wrong with her. Her Nurse has not been any use. She's all on her own. That's very wrong!'

C 'She is a young, immature girl who is in love with the idea of being in love. Her parents know what is best for her and the Nurse is right. She could have a great life with Paris: he's a keeper. She should forget about Romeo and move on.'

D 'She and Romeo are two tragic figures being destroyed by some kind of fate – something they do not understand and cannot fight against. They are moving to their deaths and nobody can stop this from happening.'

2 Give each of these responses a number in the order in which you agree with them, from 1 ('strongly agree') to 4 ('strongly disagree').

3 What are the reasons for your choices?

GETTING CLOSER – FOCUS ON DETAILS

Plot development

This is Juliet's act. Romeo exits early in Act 3 Scene 5 and we don't see him again until the beginning of Act 5. Juliet is either on stage or she is the subject of the other characters' **dialogue** (or both) for most of the act.

1 Look through Act 4 and note down the names of all the characters who appear.

    a   What do they each contribute?
    b   Which character is on stage most and says most?

2 In Act 4, several key events occur as a result of what happened in Acts 1–3. Make notes on the way each of these events is caused by something that happened earlier in the play.

 Read more about the plot of *Romeo and Juliet* in Unit 6.

Scene 1
Paris visits Friar Lawrence and they have a brief conversation about Paris's marriage to Juliet. Paris leaves and Juliet asks for the Friar's help to avoid having to marry Paris. The Friar suggests a plan involving a potion that will make Juliet appear to be dead. He tells her to be brave and stick to this plan: **'Hold, get you gone, be strong and prosperous / In this resolve'.**

Scene 2
Lord Capulet is planning the wedding. Juliet pretends to agree to marry Paris, so Capulet brings the wedding forward by 24 hours.

Scene 3
Juliet worries about what she is about to do, before finally drinking the sleeping potion as a way of escaping Paris and remaining Romeo's wife.

Scene 4
Capulet and his wife and servants are preparing for the wedding with great excitement when Paris arrives.

Scene 5
The Nurse finds Juliet in bed, apparently dead. The Nurse is joined in her grief by Lord and Lady Capulet, Friar Lawrence and Paris. The scene ends with a comic quarrel involving the servant Peter and the musicians.

What must be shall be.

Juliet: Act 4 Scene 1, line 21

ACT 4 SCENE 1: PARIS AND JULIET

Character and performance

At the beginning of Act 4 Juliet goes to Friar Lawrence to ask for his help. There she unexpectedly meets Paris. Audiences will remember Juliet's meetings with Romeo and make comparisons.

Paris: Happily met, my lady and my wife!
Juliet: That may be, sir, when I may be a wife.
Paris: That 'may be' must be, love, on Thursday next.
Juliet: What must be shall be.

Act 4 Scene 1, lines 18-21

1 How would you describe the way Paris and Juliet speak here? Are they being open with one another?

2 Working in groups, practise saying these lines in different ways.

    a   Do you think Juliet would be embarrassed, polite or horrified? Or would she react in some other way?

    b   What about Paris? Would he be seductive, over-confident or soppy? Or would his mood be entirely different?

    c   Which version do you think is the most effective way of showing an audience what the characters are thinking?

3 Paris and Juliet are using language to argue about whether or not she's going to marry him. Here's one example: '**Thy face is mine**' (line 35).

    a   What do these words tell the audience about Paris?

    b   How do you think Paris should say these words?

4 Here's a second example: '**Juliet, on Thursday early will I rouse ye; / Till then adieu, and keep this holy kiss**' (lines 42–43).

    a   How do you think Paris should kiss Juliet?

    b   How should Juliet respond?

Read more about characterisation in *Romeo and Juliet* in Unit 8.

Language, character and plot

Look closely at lines 18–34. The lines alternate quickly between Paris and Juliet, reflecting their tension and excitement.

At the beginning, Paris and Juliet take it in turns to speak, producing a series of alternating one-liners that feels a bit like a ball bouncing back and forth in a tennis rally (lines 18–26).

1 After line 26, the pattern changes. Paris speaks single lines and Juliet replies with pairs of lines (lines 26–34); then each of the two speaks three lines.

    a   How would you interpret this change of pace?
    b   How would you direct the actors to speak and move differently as the pattern of lines changes?

2 Once you have studied lines 18–34, re-read Act 1 Scene 5, lines 92–109. Then answer the following questions, writing one paragraph for each.

    a   What similarities and differences do you notice in the way in which:
        • Romeo and Juliet speak to one another in Act 1 Scene 5
        • Paris and Juliet talk in Act 4 Scene 1?
    b   How does this section of the play (Act 4 Scene 1, lines 28–43) help our understanding of the plot and Juliet's character?

Once Paris has left, Juliet declares her distress and Friar Lawrence tells her he knows about the situation: '**O Juliet, I already know thy grief**' (line 46). The language changes completely and everything slows down.

The earlier part of the scene was rapid-fire, with the characters speaking in short sentences. In contrast, the rest of the scene consists of Juliet and the Friar saying what they really mean, and using longer sentences. The first part appeared to be a comedy about getting married. In this second part, Juliet and the Friar are planning a deception in which Juliet will pretend to die. The **theme** of death has returned.

Read more about language in *Romeo and Juliet* in Unit 10.

O Juliet, I already know thy grief,
It strains me past the compass of my wits.

Friar Lawrence: Act 4 Scene 1, lines 46–47

ACT 4 SCENE 1: CHANGING IDEAS

A changing atmosphere

It would be easy just to feel sorry for Juliet and conclude that this scene is all about grief and tears. In fact there's also quite a lot of violence and blood in the language.

1 Read through the dialogue that begins at line 44 and continues to the end of the scene. While you read, make a list of all the images of illness and death.

2 In Act 4 Scene 1, lines 53-54, Juliet says:

> Do thou but call my resolution wise,
> And with this knife I'll help it presently.

The word '**presently**' means 'at once' or 'immediately', rather than 'in a little while' as it would in modern English. Which other words or phrases in her first speech create a feeling of urgency?

Juliet and the Friar: character and language

In this part of the scene Juliet gives her opinion about the Friar.

1 Read her first speech (lines 50–67)

   a   Note down those words that indicate what she thinks of him.
   b   What does her choice of words tell us about the role he plays in her life?

Contexts

In Shakespeare's day, most people thought suicide was a sin and was only committed by those who had no faith in God's mercy. It had **connotations** of shame and horror. People who committed suicide were not buried in churchyards; they were sometimes buried at crossroads, like people who had been executed for crimes. Sometimes religious authorities seized all the money and land belonging to the person who had committed suicide, leaving their family in poverty.

On the other hand, some people thought suicide could be a noble act, requiring great courage and showing personal honour. Shakespeare clearly thought it was an important issue, as there are over a dozen suicides in his plays.

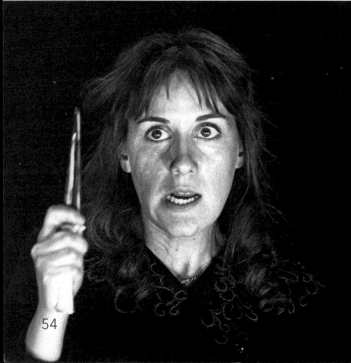

Do thou but call my resolution wise,
And with this knife I'll help it presently.

Juliet: Act 4 Scene 1, lines 53–54

2 In lines 52–54, Juliet uses repetition to make a connection between herself and the Friar.

a   What are the two words that she uses? (There's one in each of the two lines.)
b   What theme does the repetition bring out?
c   What does Juliet's response to the Friar here and elsewhere in the scene show us about Juliet herself?

Read more about language in *Romeo and Juliet* in Unit 10.

3 Juliet ends one of her speeches (lines 50–67) with a rhyming couplet:

Be not so long to speak, I long to die,
If what thou speak'st speak not of remedy.

Annotate these lines (66–67), paying close attention to Shakespeare's use of repetition and rhyme. The coloured highlighting will help you.

4 Friar Lawrence's next speech (lines 89–120) is one of the longer speeches in the play. Read through it, make sure you understand it, and then rewrite it in modern English prose.

5 Now answer the following questions. In each case, find evidence from the speech to support your interpretation.

a   What are the themes in the speech? (You might consider, for example, that his opening advice '**go home, be merry**' raises the theme of deception.)
b   What does this speech show us about the Friar? (You could start by thinking about his use of scientific language.)
c   How would you characterise the language he uses? Would you, for example, describe it as friendly, poetic, practical, down to earth, emotional, cold or something else? Or do you think it's a combination?

Text to performance

1 Get into pairs, one to act and one to direct a rehearsal of Juliet's speech in lines 77–88. Notice that she presents a series of alternatives.

a   How many times does Juliet use the word 'or' in this speech?
b   How should you use this word in a performance?
c   How would you describe the imagery that Juliet uses in this speech?

ACT 4 SCENES 2 AND 3: PROMISES AND LIES

Characterisation in Scene 2

The next scene opens with Lord Capulet giving instructions concerning preparations for the wedding.

Juliet's arrival is greeted by the Nurse, who uses a word that suggests Juliet has taken Friar Lawrence's advice.

1 Can you find the word? (If not, look back at Act 4 Scene 1, line 89.)

2 What do we learn here about Juliet's personality? Would you call her determined, cunning, headstrong or loyal? Or would you use other descriptions?

Performance in Scene 3

We are back in Juliet's bedroom for another women-only scene. Juliet talks to her mother and the Nurse and then delivers a long soliloquy.

Juliet's speeches to the Nurse and her mother are examples of dramatic irony. The Nurse and Lady Capulet think Juliet is happy to be marrying Paris but the audience knows otherwise.

1 With a partner, act out Juliet's lines 1–5 and 7–12, one of you saying the lines and the other saying what Juliet really thinks. How can you best bring out:

  a   the underlying comedy – the scene is full of misunderstandings
  b   the dramatic tension – Juliet has Friar Lawrence's potion in her pocket
  c   the issue of character – Juliet is lying, but the audience still has to sympathise with her, otherwise the play stops being a tragedy?

With the other two women gone, Juliet produces her dagger and the 'vial' (little bottle) the Friar gave her. Read Juliet's speech (lines 14–58) and note down the indirect questions (for example 'when' in line 14) and the direct questions (for example 'what' in line 18).

2 Are these questions about practical matters or philosophical issues?

3 Given your answer to this question, what do you think of Juliet's character now?

Read more about characterisation in *Romeo and Juliet* in Unit 8.

Contexts

Juliet apologises to her father (lines 16–21). She calls her disobedience a 'sin' and says 'I have learnt me to repent'. This is Church language: she means she's done wrong (sinned), realised what she's done and resolved to change (repent). Juliet knows that children are told to respect their parents in the Bible's Ten Commandments. This language is clearly intended to reassure her father.

Key terms

dramatic irony: when the audience knows something about a character or plot that a character on stage is not aware of.

tragedy: a play with an unhappy ending, usually involving the downfall of the main character.

Language form and structure

Not surprisingly, Juliet is afraid to drink the potion, but she is also afraid it won't work (that's why she keeps the dagger close at hand). She expresses this fear in a speech full of frightening imagery.

1 Examine the imagery of Juliet's soliloquy. There are two examples in this table.

Quotation	Comments about how the image works
'faint cold fear thrills through my veins / That almost freezes up the heat of life' (lines 15–16)	*Fear personified? Fear is like an icy liquid flowing through Juliet's veins and freezing her warm blood.*
'vault, / To whose foul mouth no healthsome air breathes in' (lines 33–34)	*Tomb (vault) personified? It will be sealed up like a closed mouth, trapping stagnant, deadly and unhealthy air inside.*

Examine these examples in the same way:

a   'bloody Tybalt, yet but green in earth, / Lies fest'ring in his shroud' (lines 42–43)

b   'shrieks like mandrakes' (line 47)

c   'pluck the mangled Tybalt from his shroud' (line 52)

d   'with some great kinsman's bone, / As with a club' (lines 53–54)

e   'that did spit his body / Upon a rapier's point' (lines 56–57)

Read more about language in *Romeo and Juliet* in Unit 10.

2 Choose three of these images and write a paragraph about them. Here is an example.

Learning checkpoint

Look back over the unit. Then write a paragraph (or more) in response to the following question. You should use the notes you have made so far in this unit to help you.

Q How do you think Shakespeare presents Juliet at this point in the play?

How will I know I've done this well?

✔   Include your own original and thoughtful interpretation.

✔   Make use of at least one quotation that you explain fully.

✔   Explore the way the audience might respond to Juliet.

✔   Use accurate spelling and clear, well-punctuated sentences.

Juliet refers to 'shrieks like mandrakes' torn out of the earth, / That living mortals hearing them run mad'. This is an image of madness, violence and death. Mandrakes were plants that people believed grew beneath gallows (where people were hanged) and shrieked when they were pulled up.

ACT 4 SCENES 4 AND 5: COMEDY AND TRAGEDY

Themes and theatricality in Scene 4

This is a light-hearted scene about domestic practicalities, with Capulet hurrying everyone along: **'stir, stir, stir!'** (line 3). He means both 'get a move on!' but also 'stir that saucepan!' Capulet is a great one for repeating himself: he says **'make haste'** several times.

1 There are hints of seriousness though:

    a   Are the spices in the opening line an innocent reference to the kitchen or a subtle reminder of Friar Lawrence collecting herbs in Act 3 Scene 2?

    b   What does the dialogue between Juliet's parents mean (lines 9–13)?

2 There is a technical term to describe the fact that this whole scene has a hidden serious side, which the characters are unaware of. What is it? (We used it earlier to describe the first part of Scene 3.)

Theatricality and performance in Scene 5

Act 4 Scene 5 begins with a silent, unmoving Juliet on an empty stage. There are then no fewer than five entrances, one after another.

1 List the entrances in order (the first one has been given as an example):

    A   The Nurse _____

    B   _____

    C   _____

    D   _____

    E   _____

2 With Juliet not speaking or moving, the stage is full of people we've learned not to trust. Discuss what the audience might make of their emotions.

3 Look at the language these mourners use to express themselves.

    a   How would you describe it? You may wish to use some of the words and phrases in the word bank.

    b   Write three sentences about the impression the mourners will make on an audience.

heartfelt	poetic
artificial	in character
unexpected	

A key technique Shakespeare uses throughout this scene is repetition. Characters repeat themselves. They also repeat words that other characters have used.

 4 What effects do you think Shakespeare is trying to achieve through this use of repetition?

Explore the Nurse's response to Juliet's death in Act 4 Scene 5 on Cambridge Elevate.

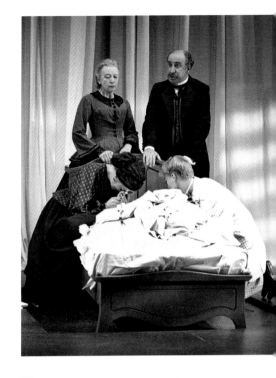

Plot and structure

On three occasions in Act 4, the plot changes from tragedy to comedy. There is an example here at the end of Scene 5. Juliet's parents believe she is really dead and Lord Capulet is grief-stricken: '**All things that we ordainèd festival, / Turn from their office to black funeral**'. Yet, when the mourners have gone, the scene ends with a comic quarrel between the servant Peter and the Musicians.

The end of Scene 5 (beginning at line 96) may remind you of the Capulet servants at the beginning of the play. Mixing high tragedy with comedy is an example of **juxtaposition**.

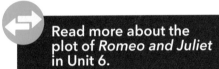

Read more about the plot of *Romeo and Juliet* in Unit 6.

 1 Do you think Shakespeare juxtaposed tragedy and comedy in this way because:

a   it gave the audience a break from the tragic events (without this, the play would be too miserable)

b   it made the tragedy greater by providing a contrast

c   it showed that individual tragedy took place in the context of a wider society

d   it gave the common folk who stood in front of the stage something to laugh at?

Key terms

juxtaposition: the placement of two ideas or things near each other to invite comparison or contrast.

All things that we ordainèd festival,
Turn from their office to black funeral:
Our instruments to melancholy bells,
Our wedding cheer to a sad burial
    feast ...

Capulet: Act 4 Scene 5, lines 84–87

GETTING IT INTO WRITING

Writing about Juliet's character

Character is an important aspect of studying *Romeo and Juliet*. Review the places where you've looked at Juliet's character in this unit, then answer the following question.

1 Explore how Shakespeare presents Juliet's character in Act 4.

To do this well, you need to write about:

a Scenes 1–3, where **she speaks**

b Scenes 4–5, where **she is spoken about** (which could prove important to your argument)

c how Shakespeare presents Juliet's thoughts and feelings at this stage of the play

d Shakespeare's use of language and imagery

e how the action may be presented in performance.

What evidence is there in the text to support your views?

Here are four sample openings to give you ideas for getting started:

Complete this assignment on Cambridge Elevate.

Shakespeare shows that Juliet develops from being an innocent thirteen-year-old girl to a young woman who shows great determination and courage and is ready to sacrifice herself for love. Anyone would admire her and be amazed at the journey she has made since the start of the play. She is even prepared to take a potion to appear dead so that she does not have to marry Paris.

Juliet begins the play surrounded by a caring and supportive family. Her Nurse is her best friend and her father wishes only the best for her. Towards the end of the play Shakespeare shows that she is ready to leave all that she once valued – her family, her home, her social position in one of the great families of Verona, her inheritance (for she will inherit her father's fortune when he dies) – to follow her love to the ends of the earth. This is self-indulgent at best. At worst it is just plain stupid.

Shakespeare presents a young girl who does not really grow up. She falls in love instantly and is then given to outbursts of grief and anger when she turns on people who are only trying to look out for her. In just a few days, she lies and blackmails to get what she wants. She wants too much, too soon. When she is given the opportunity to do something positive, she worries about how it might go wrong.

In the character of Juliet, Shakespeare has created a truly tragic figure. The audience knows that her short life will end in her sudden death and that her love will be 'star-crossed'. It is symbolic that her birthday is on 1st August (Lammas Eve, the day before the Harvest Festival in Elizabethan England). She will not live to see the 'harvest' (her marriage to Romeo) fulfilled. She may be intelligent, practical and determined but she is also subject to a fate she can neither understand nor control: a fate that will cut short her life. This is what makes her tragic. When given the opportunity of being reunited with Romeo, she is prepared to act, no matter what the consequences.

GETTING FURTHER

Performing Scene 5

This is the longest scene in Act 4 and it begins with the Nurse, who has been sent by Capulet to wake his daughter. She makes jokes about Juliet's wedding night.

This is a difficult scene for actors to get right. The Nurse has to be full of life and laughter. She assumes it's a wedding day, as though the play were a comedy called *Paris and Juliet*, with a happy ending now in view.

1 Would you direct it with:

   a   Juliet in full view, lying on the bed
   b   curtains around the bed which the Nurse draws (at line 12)
   c   the Nurse trying to make the audience laugh?

2 When Lady Capulet enters, we have a repeat of the beginning of Scene 3, with the three women in Juliet's bedroom. How would you organise the characters to bring out that connection?

3 Read this part of the scene (lines 1–17) and discuss how best to interpret it.

4 You have been asked to make a film of this scene. You can use up to 12 different shots. These can include close-up, panning and tracking shots and overhead shots. You can also include a very short piece of script, consisting of short phrases from lines 1–17 which you think are key to the action.

   a   Storyboard and, if you can, film the sequence.
   b   Now compare your version with those of:
      • Franco Zeffirelli (1968), starting from the shot of the cat by the well (the second appearance the cat makes in the film)
      • Baz Luhrmann (1996), starting from the overhead shot of Juliet on her bed.
   c   Which do you think is the most dramatic? What aspects make you think this?

5

Act 5: Ends and endings

How does Shakespeare close the play in Act 5?

Your progress in this unit:

- understand and explain Shakespeare's choice of ending for the play
- explore the way Shakespeare presents the deaths of Romeo and Juliet
- analyse Shakespeare's use of language and structure and its impact on the audience
- consider the ideas in Act 5 and how they could be presented in performance
- develop your written response skills.

GETTING STARTED – THE PLAY AND YOU

Do you believe in fate?

This is the act in which the lovers die, the moment the whole **tragedy** has been relentlessly moving towards. Why do they end up dying?

Romeo blames astrology, echoing the Prologue: '**I defy you, stars!**' (Act 5 Scene 1, line 24).

Friar Lawrence blames fortune '**Unhappy fortune**' (Act 5 Scene 2, line 17) and '**chance**' (Act 5 Scene 3, line 146). He later develops this idea further.

A greater power than we can contradict
Hath thwarted our intents.

Act 5 Scene 3, lines 153–154

1 What do you think Friar Lawrence means when he says a '**greater power**' has brought about these events?

2 Do you believe in a power or pattern that makes things happen, good or bad? Can you describe this power?

GETTING CLOSER – FOCUS ON DETAILS

Plot development

If Act 4 was Juliet's act, Act 5 is at least initially Romeo's. He is at the centre of Scene 1 and the beginning of Scene 3, and he is the subject of the **dialogue** in Scene 2. Clearly the relationship between the lovers is the heart of the play. It's what we want to know about, and it's what makes everything happen. Yet, although this is famously a play about love, Act 5 is mainly about death.

1 Make a list of the people who die in this act.

2 Read the plot summary for Act 5 and remind yourself of Acts 1–4. How much of the play do Romeo and Juliet actually spend together? (Hint: it's not a lot of time!)

a   Less than 10%
b   10–25%
c   25–50%

Answer: it's about 13% (when they're on stage speaking together). They don't see each other alive after Act 3 Scene 5. Although they share the stage in the final scene, there is no dialogue between them.

3 What do you think the percentage answer suggests about the lovers' journey in the play and the way it is presented?

Scene 1

Romeo has had a dream in which he was dead but was brought back to life by Juliet. His servant Balthasar brings him news of Juliet's death. He decides to return to Verona and commit suicide in the Capulet family vault (tomb) where Juliet has been buried. He visits an apothecary (pharmacist) to buy poison.

Scene 2

Friar John returns to Friar Lawrence, having failed to deliver Friar Lawrence's letter to Romeo. Friar Lawrence decides to go to the Capulet vault immediately.

Scene 3

Paris is in the churchyard, outside the Capulet vault. Then Romeo and Balthasar enter, to open up the vault. Paris hears Romeo's voice and knows him only as Tybalt's killer who has returned illegally from exile. They fight and Romeo kills Paris. At the request of the dying Paris, Romeo takes his body into the tomb to lie near Juliet. Romeo then swallows the poison and dies. Friar Lawrence enters and finds both young men dead and Juliet waking up. He tries to persuade her to leave and then runs away. Juliet sees that Romeo is dead and stabs herself. The Watch (police) enter and arrest Balthasar and Friar Lawrence. The Prince and Juliet's parents enter, followed by Lord Montague, who says that his wife (Romeo's mother) has died of grief. The Prince begins an enquiry. Friar Lawrence explains what has happened. Montague and Capulet promise to end their quarrel. The Prince says he will punish some and pardon others.

ACT 5 SCENE 1: SETTINGS, CONTEXTS AND NEW CHARACTERS

Romeo's 'strange dream'

Scene 1 opens with Romeo's **soliloquy**. He's had a dream and interprets it in a hopeful way, which makes him feel happy. In the 16th century, people believed that, if understood correctly, dreams could foretell the future.

Romeo and Mercutio discussed dreams in Act 1 Scene 4. Mercutio suggested then that they were meaningless, '**the children of an idle brain**' and '**fantasy**' (Act 1 Scene 4, lines 97–98).

1 Look at the references to sleep, dreams and spirits in Act 5 Scene 1, lines 1–11.

   a   What does Romeo think about dreams in general? And what does he think about this new dream in particular?

   b   How does Shakespeare use **irony** in Romeo's account of his dream?

Unequal relationships

When Balthasar enters, Romeo is excited: '**News from Verona!**' (line 12). Unless Balthasar is one of the Montague servingmen who got into a quarrel with Sampson and Gregory in Act 1 Scene 1 (as some editions suggest), we haven't met him before. To find out who he is, the audience has to interpret the dialogue. For example when Balthasar arrives, Romeo fires a lot of short, urgent questions at him. Balthasar, knowing that he has to break dreadful news to Romeo, is much more polite and cautious in his response.

1 What do you notice about the way Balthasar and Romeo speak to one another?

2 What other features of their dialogue can you identify?

3 What is it about their way of speaking that shows the nature of their relationship? You might begin by looking at who speaks first, who gives the instructions and commands and how the two characters address each other.

4 What does Romeo's response to Balthasar's news tell us about Romeo?

5 Compare Romeo and Balthasar's conversation with the one Juliet had with the Nurse in Act 3 Scene 2, when she heard about Tybalt's death and Romeo's exile. Note the similarities and differences in the way the two employers and employees act and speak to each other.

The Apothecary's shop

After the **duologue**, Balthasar leaves and Romeo makes a long speech, saying that he plans to commit suicide and describing an apothecary's shop, where he thinks he can buy poison. He then describes the man and his shop in detail. This is another example of Shakespeare providing scenery through language. The last part of the scene takes place in the shop. After Romeo's description, we already know what it looks like.

1 Read Romeo's speech at lines 35–56. What does it tell us about Romeo and the world he lives in?

News from Verona! How now, Balthasar?

Romeo: Act 5 Scene 1, line 12

64

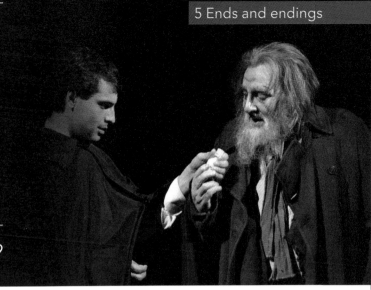

Put this in any liquid thing you will
And drink it off, and if you had the strength
Of twenty men, it would dispatch you straight.

The Apothecary: Act 5 Scene 1, lines 77–79

The plot is gathering pace and the audience is excited:

- Juliet is drugged and left inside the family vault.
- Friar Lawrence has sent a letter, which is chasing Romeo.
- Romeo is about to buy poison and is planning his own death.

Then everything stops to allow Romeo to describe a shop and a shopkeeper. Many critics have wondered why Shakespeare does this.

2 Would you cut some or all of Romeo's speech about the Apothecary's shop? Try to justify your decision.

You should:

a **either** explain what the soliloquy contributes to the play at this stage
b **or** explain how cutting it would help the performance.

 Explore the Apothecary scene on Cambridge Elevate.

Apothecaries are a part of Shakespeare's world that has changed. As a result, the director, actor and designer have to think about how to present him effectively.

3 Would you costume this character:

a in a dirty robe embroidered with star signs
b in a white coat like a modern pharmacist
c as a drug dealer?

4 You are an actor planning your performance as the Apothecary. He speaks four times and only has six and a half lines. His longest speech is a simple instruction: '**Put this in any liquid thing you will / And drink it off, and if you had the strength / Of twenty men, it would dispatch you straight.**' Yet, brief or not, he's an interesting character and essential to the plot.

a What character in recent films or television programmes could you model him on? Remember, he deals in drugs and sells poison. He has studied mysterious things that combine science and magic.
b How do you think you could use your brief appearance to make an impression on the audience?

5 Look at how Romeo speaks first of all **about** the Apothecary, and then **to** him. What do we learn about:

a the Apothecary
b Mantua
c Romeo?

 Read more about the context of *Romeo and Juliet* in Unit 7.

ACT 5 SCENES 2 AND 3: CHARACTER AND SETTING

How Scene 2 advances the plot and themes

In this short scene, Friar Lawrence is horrified to learn that Friar John has not succeeded in delivering to Romeo the letter explaining the secret plan.

1 Make a note of how each one contributes to the plot, as in this example.

> Friar Lawrence asks Friar John to 'get me an iron crow' (line 21). This is a crowbar, which he intends to use to break into the Capulets' vault and rescue Juliet, who will wake up soon.

The language in this scene also features certain **themes**. For example Friar John tells Friar Lawrence that '**my speed to Mantua there was stayed** [delayed]' (line 12). This plays on the theme of 'fast versus slow', which Shakespeare explores throughout the play.

2 Can you identify two other themes in this scene?

Characterisation in Scene 3

In Scene 3, Paris and Romeo meet for the first and last time. These two characters have several things in common:

- both are young men
- both wanted to marry Juliet
- both now believe her to be dead.

The scene opens with Paris making a promise to Juliet:

> The obsequies that I for thee will keep
> Nightly shall be to strew thy grave and weep.

Paris: Act 5 Scene 3, lines 16–17

Contexts

A burial vault is a tomb, usually built underneath a church or cemetery. Vaults were normally for rich families. They often had a stone slab at the entrance for protection. The word '**monument**' suggests the purpose of the construction is to remind everyone of the Capulet family's importance.

1 Read Paris's short soliloquy at lines 12–17. How would you describe his response to Juliet's death? You might want to use one or more of the **adjectives** in the word bank.

heartbroken	melodramatic	lost
formal	conventional	poetic
immature		

Romeo and Balthasar arrive and they have a short conversation (lines 22–44).

2 How does the way Romeo treats Balthasar compare with the way Paris treated his page earlier in the same scene? Draw attention to similarities and differences in the way Romeo and Paris speak and their use of **imagery** and themes.

Key terms

adjective: a word that describes a noun.

Read more about characterisation in *Romeo and Juliet* in Unit 8.

Here is an example of how to start:

Paris arrives at the tomb with flowers, which he proceeds to scatter while speaking poetically. This is quite different from Romeo, who arrives with a mattock and 'wrenching iron' and starts breaking open the tomb. This suggests …

Shakespeare often gives characters lines showing they have misunderstood some things and are being deceptive about others, so we have to listen, watch and read with care.

3 Romeo explains to Balthasar his reasons for visiting Juliet's tomb at lines 28–32. Do you believe him?

4 Paris gives the reason for Juliet's supposed death at lines 50–51. What is it and what does this misunderstanding tell us?

Production and theatricality

Scene 3 begins in a churchyard. Romeo breaks into the Capulet tomb and, after killing Paris, takes Paris's body into the tomb, close to Juliet.

1 Imagine that you are directing Scene 3.

    a   What exactly is Romeo breaking into?
    b   What does he do with Paris's body?
    c   Is the scene still in the churchyard or have we gone inside a building of some kind?

2 Look at these images from the Luhrmann (A) and Zeffirelli (B) films of *Romeo and Juliet*. How do the settings differ?

ACT 5 SCENE 3: LANGUAGE AND THE AUDIENCE'S EXPECTATIONS

The play's effect is partly achieved through its structure. This includes setting up the audience's expectations and then either fulfilling them or springing a surprise. Sometimes expectations are set up by language. Certain themes and ideas recur, and so do certain words and events.

1 Romeo's last words are: '**Thus with a kiss I die**' (line 120).

   a How does Romeo's death link back to his first meeting with Juliet?

   b How would you describe Romeo's death? You might want to use some of the words in the word bank.

sad   tragic   ironic   poetic   romantic   predictable

The next section of Scene 3 begins with Friar Lawrence being brought in by Balthasar and ends with him failing to persuade Juliet to leave.

2 How does Shakespeare use language when the Friar is talking to Romeo's servant, to himself and to the awakening Juliet? Note down the differences and comment on the reasons for them. You could begin as in this example.

> At first Friar Lawrence speaks to Balthasar in hasty, short speeches, like someone in a hurry or frightened. Then …

3 Before he runs away from the vault, Friar Lawrence comes up with yet another plan. What is this plan? Why doesn't he wait for Juliet to respond to it?

Thus with a kiss I die.

Romeo: Act 5 Scene 3, line 120

Language and character

This is Juliet's last scene. Romeo and Paris are already dead, so both her marriage options have gone. In addition, her family assume that she herself is already dead. An audience might feel that she has nothing left to lose. She has very few lines left to say. Count them and think about what an actor has to achieve with these few lines.

1 Analyse Juliet's first speech (lines 148–150).

   a   What is the significance of the adjective '**comfortable**' and what does it tell you about her relationship with Friar Lawrence?

   b   What does Juliet mean when she says '**I do remember well where I should be; / And there I am**'? Relate this apparently simple statement of location to the play's theme of fate.

   c   She twice asks after Romeo. What effect do you think this repeated question will have on an audience? What does the term '**lord**' tell you about their relationship?

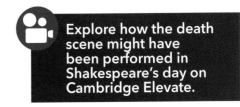

Explore how the death scene might have been performed in Shakespeare's day on Cambridge Elevate.

Production and theatricality

As Juliet dies, the audience hears the sound of the approaching Watch. The Watch represents the police force of Verona, which is a town in Italy. However, these three individuals are actually based on Shakespeare's own experience of the forces of law and order in 16th-century London and Stratford.

When members of the Watch appear In Shakespeare's other plays, they are comic, poorly educated characters.

1 Read lines 168–201 and list all the things the Watch do and say, commenting on each one's literal meaning and its significance.

2 Elsewhere in *Romeo and Juliet* short scenes with servants are comic. Is this section of Scene 3 comic?

3 What evidence can you find in the text to support your view?

4 Look at the way Shakespeare has written for the Watchmen. What does it suggest about the way he expected them to be played?

5 How should the Watchmen be costumed and played – for example as policemen, beefeaters or Robocop? Explain the reasons for your decision by describing their role in Scene 3 and the mood and tone in this section.

Led in by Paris's page, the Watch have arrested Balthasar and Friar Lawrence offstage. With the Prince on stage, the wheels of justice start to turn. This is interrupted by Juliet's parents and then Romeo's father.

TRUTH AND RECONCILIATION

Themes and ideas

Lady Capulet announces that the town is alive with gossip about the three young people we've just seen die violent deaths. Her speech (lines 191–193) reminds us that the play is not only about Romeo and Juliet but also about an entire community.

When Lord Capulet sees his daughter's dead body, he refers to Romeo.

1 What does he call him?

2 Which of Juliet's soliloquies does this name recall? (It's in Act 2 Scene 2.)

Romeo's father is in conversation with the Prince. Within a few lines, we have the words '**son**', '**heir**', '**liege**' and '**wife**'. These are all to do with relationships in families and society. Now comes the news that Romeo's mother has just died.

3 Why has Shakespeare included Lady Montague's death in the plot, and why here? Do you think it is because he wants to show:

    a   the power of family relationships
    b   that older people in the play also have emotional lives
    c   that parents can feel emotion for their children?

Read more about ideas in *Romeo and Juliet* in Unit 9.

Production and theatricality

There are three dead bodies on stage and, like any detective inspector, the Prince needs to establish whether this is a murder enquiry. Friar Lawrence offers to speak as a witness. Remember: with the lovers dead, only **he** understands the mystery.

The Friar delivers one of the two longest speeches in the play. It's clearly important; yet it contains no new information for the audience.

1 If it isn't to inform the audience, why do you think Shakespeare put this long speech here?

    a   How does the Prince respond to what Friar Lawrence says?
    b   Luhrmann and Zeffirelli both cut the Friar's speech in their films. (*Shakespeare in Love* does so as well, by the way.) If you were directing the play, would you cut it or keep it? Give your reasons.

Having heard three witnesses and examined a document, the Prince calls the lovers' fathers forward, like a judge ordering the accused men to stand for sentencing.

2 In the Prince's speech at lines 286–295, whom does he call guilty?

    a   What reasons does he give to justify his decision?
    b   When he mentions '**kinsmen**', whom is he referring to? What theme does his use of the word remind us of?
    c   How would you interpret his phrase '**all are punished**'? (It could mean different things. You should show in your answer that you understand this.)
    d   Capulet and Montague shake hands in a gesture of reconciliation. What stages does this short peace process go through and what are the elements of the peace treaty? The first three stages are shown in part. What are the fourth and fifth stages?

    1. *Capulet offers to shake hands with Montague.*

    2. *Capulet offers Montague …*

    3. *Montague promises Capulet to …*

3 While the two fathers are shaking hands, one mother is offstage and dead, and the other is on stage but silent. What does this situation tell you?

Explore the ending of the play on Cambridge Elevate.

    a Is Lady Capulet overwhelmed by grief? Or is she holding back from the reconciliation as though still hostile?

    b Are the fathers heartbroken by the tragedy? Or are they going through a formal ceremony of grief because the Prince is watching them?

4 Finally, the Prince ends the play with a short speech (lines 305–310). What form does Shakespeare use for this passage? Is it in prose or verse?

    a If it's in verse, is it blank verse or rhyming verse? If it is rhyming verse, what is the rhyme scheme?

    b Why do you think Shakespeare has written it in this form?

5 Write a paragraph explaining whom you think the Prince is going to pardon and whom punish.

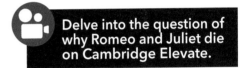

Delve into the question of why Romeo and Juliet die on Cambridge Elevate.

    a Explain the evidence in the text that suggests these will be his decisions.

    b How would your own judgement differ from his?

Learning checkpoint

This act ends the play, so it has to pull all the storylines together and conclude the plot. To understand Act 5, you need to be able to see it in the context of the play as a whole. It may be helpful to consider questions such as:

✔ What happened earlier in the play that caused the events in Act 5?

✔ What do we learn about the characters?

✔ What are the themes and ideas?

✔ How does the use of language connect this act to earlier acts?

✔ What is new in this act?

All are punished.

Prince: Act 5 Scene 3, line 295

GETTING IT INTO WRITING

Themes and ideas

Throughout the play, the question of why things happen keeps coming up. There are many references to fate, fortune and the influence of the stars:

- Romeo talks about '**This day's black fate**' (Act 3 Scene 1, line 110).
- There are 12 references to '**fortune**', starting in Act 1 Scene 2 and ending in Act 5 Scene 3.
- The first reference to stars and astrology is in the Prologue and the last is in the final scene.

Does this mean that Shakespeare believed in fate? Re-read your notes, and think about what characters say, what they do and what just seems to happen without anyone planning it.

 Complete this assignment on Cambridge Elevate.

1 Collect different quotations from the play on the themes of fate, fortune and the influence of the stars.

2 How does Shakespeare present the idea of fate in Act 5 Scene 3, the final scene of the play?

3 How do you respond to the theme of fate in the play as a whole?

After you have drafted an answer to this question, turn to the exam preparation section, where you will find some sample answers to this question, together with examiner-style comments.

Do not simply copy what you find, as this won't help you practise writing or improve your exam skills. Instead, notice what qualities the comments draw attention to, and see how you can improve your own answer using their guidance.

Most people would say that *Romeo and Juliet* is about falling in love. As you've seen, it certainly is about that. However, it's also about death and dying. Look back over Act 5, and review your notes on Acts 1–4 as well. Think about the different ways in which people (apart from the lovers) die and the reasons for their deaths. Remember that several other people die, from Tybalt to Lady Montague.

4 Now consider the theme of death in Romeo's soliloquy, Act 5 Scene 3, lines 74–120.

- **a** How does Romeo's speech contribute to the theme of death in the play as a whole?
- **b** How does he use language and imagery? You might want to consider the following:
  - Romeo actually talks to Death as though to a person: what's this **poetic device** called?
  - He talks about Death as a rival lover: what does that make you think?
  - He ends his speech with a kiss: what does that remind you of? And what impression does it make here?

This day's black fate on moe days doth depend ...

Romeo: Act 3 Scene 1, line 110

GETTING FURTHER

Whose tragedy is it?

The play is called '**the tragedy of Romeo and Juliet**'. Yet at the end of the play the Prince declares that this was the story of '**Juliet and her Romeo**'.

1 Do you think one of the lovers is more important in the play? If so, which – and in what way?

2 Re-read your notes, especially those to do with the lovers, then consider whether or not Juliet is the central character.

   a   Think about Juliet's importance to the plot and to the play's themes and ideas.
   b   You should also consider how her character develops during the course of the play, from the opening Prologue to the Prince's concluding speech.

3 In pairs, write a letter to 'Juliet, Verona'. Then swap and then write responses to one another's letters. You could write about:

   a   the problems in the play (you might want to ask Juliet about her actions and feelings, or comment on your responses as a member of the audience)
   b   other problems, real or imagined (how does writing a letter to someone differ from writing in your diary?).

In Shakespeare's romantic comedies, there are misunderstandings and relationships run into difficulties but it all works out by the end. Many of the elements of *Romeo and Juliet* are present in these comic plays.

4 What would have to change to make *Romeo and Juliet* a comedy?

You might be tempted just to say 'instead of dying, they would get married' or 'the audience would have to laugh more often'. But it would take more than some extra scenes with the Nurse or Mercutio to turn it into a comedy. You'll also need to rethink much of the plot and rebalance the themes.

Contexts

A statue of Juliet that stands in Verona has been so damaged by tourists touching it that the city is having a replacement made. Letters, often addressed to 'Juliet, Verona', continue to arrive in the city from all over the world, asking for Juliet's advice about relationships. All the letters are answered by volunteers.

6

Plot and structure

How does Shakespeare take the audience on a journey in *Romeo and Juliet*?

Your progress in this unit:
- understand and explain the structure and development of the plot
- interpret the theatricality and dramatic impact of the play
- explore how the language and action of the play develops
- write about plot, structure and theatricality.

PLOT

Romeo and Juliet is not a true story, but it may have been influenced by one or more real-life stories as well as by several works of fiction. There really were two Italian families with similar names to Montague and Capulet (Montecchi and Cappelletti), who were engaged in a political fight, probably around 1300. There were several Latin and Greek **myths** that resembled this story, and Shakespeare may have learned about them at school. In the 15th century, an Italian author wrote a story with a similar plot, and Shakespeare may have read an English translation and then used it as the basis of his play.

The central story of *Romeo and Juliet* is probably one of the best-known stories in the world. It can be summarised very simply (see panel).

 Watch a plot summary of the play on Cambridge Elevate.

A boy and a girl fall in love at first sight. They do not know it, but they come from families who hate each other bitterly. They love each other so much that they get married, even though they know it's very risky. Everything begins to go wrong for them. Finally, each commits suicide because they think the other is already dead. In one case that's true; in the other it's a tragic misunderstanding. The two families are both left grieving.

SUB-PLOTS

The central story in a play is known as the main plot. As we have seen, *Romeo and Juliet*'s main plot focuses on the two young lovers. Shakespeare gives his play more depth by adding other storylines. These are known as the sub-plots (meaning that they are 'underneath', or 'less important than', the main plot). In *Romeo and Juliet* five of these additional stories are about:

- Mercutio and his relationship with Romeo and Benvolio
- Tybalt and his desire to cause trouble and keep the family feud going
- Capulet and Lady Capulet and their wish to marry Juliet off to Paris
- The Nurse and her role in Juliet's marriage to Romeo
- Friar Lawrence and his desire to heal the division between the Montagues and the Capulets.

DEVELOP AND REVISE

1 In groups, take turns to add sentences to the short plot outline in the panel until you have a version of *Romeo and Juliet* that you think covers the entire play.

2 Compare your group's version with what other groups have written.

3 Use your summary as source material for a storyboard of the play in 10–12 frames. Create a picture brief and caption for each frame that explains what is happening. Include text from the play in your caption. You can use this example to get you started:

Frame 1	Frame 2
Picture brief: Image of the brawl Caption: 'Down with the Capulets! Down with the Montagues!'	
Frame 3	**Frame 4**

4 Now turn to the sub-plots. Pick one of the five listed earlier, and trace it through the play. Discuss or write about what this particular sub-plot adds to the drama and its importance in connecting with, and telling us more about, the main plot.

CLASSICAL TRAGEDY

A **tragedy** is a specific type of play with its roots in ancient Greek drama. When *Romeo and Juliet* was first published around 1597, the title page called it 'a tragedy'. In Greek tragedy, there are certain key features that an audience expected to see:

- The **protagonist** was important and powerful. They were of noble birth and often ruled countries or were in government.
- The protagonist and others died at the end of the play. Some of those deaths were deserved because of what the characters had done. In other cases, innocent characters were caught up in events and could not escape.
- The death of the protagonist was a result of a basic weakness in their character. Sometimes this was shown by their making a key mistake, which was an error of judgement.
- Once they had made that initial mistake, disaster could not be avoided.
- Often a character's good intentions would turn out badly and increase the tragedy. This was called a 'reversal of fortune'.
- The protagonist was attractive in many ways so the audience could sympathise with them and feel sad at the end, rather than just being pleased to see them get the punishment they deserved.
- Often there was a character (or group of characters) called a Chorus who commented on the action of the play. The Chorus was not directly involved in the action. He (or they) would keep the audience informed about what was happening.

 Key terms

protagonist: the central character in a play, film or book.

HOW IS *ROMEO AND JULIET* A TRAGEDY?

Tragedy went badly out of fashion for several hundred years; old ones weren't performed and new ones weren't written. But they became very popular again in Shakespeare's day. Crowds flocked to watch tragedies, expecting lots of exciting action, blood and violence.

Shakespeare wanted to give his theatre company a play that would earn money, but he didn't just follow a popular trend. He kept many of the main, expected ingredients of tragedy, but in *Romeo and Juliet* he added a couple of surprises:

- He had **two** tragic figures at the heart of his tragedy, not one.
- His protagonists were nobles, but not powerful figures. They were not leaders or decision-makers (such as kings or generals) but young, innocent and inexperienced.

However, Romeo and Juliet **do** follow the expected tragic journey from happiness, through suffering, towards death. There is also blood and violence in the play, as when Romeo brutally kills Tybalt. Perhaps most importantly, the audience feel great sadness at the way events turn out at the end of the play.

Facing up to the inevitable

The Chorus makes it obvious from the opening speech of the play that the story will end in death. He repeats the message several times, using phrases such as '**with their death**', '**death-marked love**' and '**their children's end**'.

The action begins with a quarrel that quickly develops between the Capulet and Montague servants. The threatening atmosphere creates a sense of tragic inevitability. The lovers are optimistic, but the audience knows that things won't end well.

For never was a story of more woe
Than this of Juliet and her Romeo.

Prince: Act 5 Scene 3, lines 309–310

Is *Romeo and Juliet* really a comedy?

Although *Romeo and Juliet* is best known as a tragedy, it does have some funny episodes. These are often emphasised on stage. For example the Nurse is often played as a comic character whose earthy humour comes across strongly in key scenes. Mercutio's sexual joking also amuses the audience. The Capulet servants are entertaining while they are preparing for the party.

THE FIVE-ACT STRUCTURE

All Shakespeare's plays were divided into five acts for publication. Within each act, there are usually a number of scenes. Shakespeare uses the structure of the play to highlight the theme of conflict: a particular scene often contrasts strongly with the one that follows it – in a way that creates powerful drama. For example in Act 3 the scene where Romeo is banished is immediately followed by Juliet, alone, looking forward to her blissful time with Romeo. She is completely unaware of what has happened to her husband, but the audience knows the full story. This is an example of dramatic irony.

Audiences will be aware of changes of scene, because of the entrances and exits of characters (and, in modern theatre, sometimes alterations of scenery and lighting). But the significance of acts is far less obvious to audiences than it is to readers. Nevertheless, in *Romeo and Juliet* the five-act structure is very important. Shakespeare builds big dramatic episodes in Acts 1, 3 and 5 and contrasts them with quieter or more light-hearted scenes. This is how he reduces the tension, before building it up again very quickly.

The speed of the action

The play begins on Sunday morning and ends just before daybreak on the following Thursday. In that time, Romeo and Juliet meet, fall in love, marry and die. As the Prince says at the end, '**never was a story of more woe / Than this of Juliet and her Romeo.**' By fitting the story into four days, Shakespeare maintains a very rapid pace. For the audience, watching the play can be a breathless, exciting experience.

DEVELOP AND REVISE

1 Look through the play and find two sharply contrasting scenes. On a sticky note, write down as many contrasts between the two scenes as you can find. Put the sticky note up for display on the classroom wall.

2 There are 24 scenes in the play. Take one each. Summarise your scene in a short sentence. Then place these in order on the classroom wall to create a timeline for the play.

3 Add a picture (either one you have drawn or one you have cut out from a magazine), which you think captures the essence of your summary.

4 Challenge yourself further by reducing each scene to a key word or short headline.

7

Context, setting, stagecraft, theatricality and performance

How does Shakespeare bring the characters and action alive?

Your progress in this unit:
- Compare the views of Shakespeare's audience with those of an audience in the 21st century
- Understand and interpret the different contexts of productions
- Explore the ways in which action can be presented on stage
- Analyse the relationship between language and stage action
- Research and write about the conditions under which performance took place.

IN SHAKESPEARE'S THEATRE

When 16th- and 17th-century audiences watched Shakespeare's plays being performed at London theatres including the Curtain and the Globe, they had a very different experience from what you might expect in a modern theatre.

These were some of the differences:

- All female roles were played by boys. Women were not allowed on the English stage until half a century after Shakespeare's death.
- Performances took place in the open air, in broad daylight. Dawn, dusk and night had to be created by Shakespeare's words and the audience's imagination. For instance at the beginning of Act 2 Scene 3 Friar Lawrence describes the early morning sunlight and the clouds at sunrise.

- The stage had no scenery and few props. Again, Shakespeare used the characters' words to make clear to his audience where the action took place. For example Lord Capulet creates the atmosphere of a room full of dancers when he announces that '**the room is grown too hot**' and orders the servants to '**quench**' (put out) the fire (Act 1 Scene 5, line 27).
- There was no curtain between the audience and the main part of the stage.
- Food and drink were on sale during the performance and the audience could be rowdy.
- Poorer people stood on the ground around the stage and so were called **groundlings**.
- There were no tickets: people simply put money in a box on their way in. This is why theatres today have a 'box office'.

These were some of the similarities:

- The actors dressed up in costumes. These tended to be contemporary outfits, as they are in some modern productions.
- The audience was grouped around three sides of the stage. Well-off audience members paid extra to sit in the better seats.

 Key terms

props: 'properties'; objects and items that help to set the scene in a play.

groundlings: poorer audience members who stood on the ground around the stage, in Shakespeare's time.

DEVELOP AND REVISE

Re-read the 'Contexts' boxes from Units 1–5.

1 Talk with a partner about what it might have been like to attend a performance of *Romeo and Juliet* at the Globe Theatre in Shakespeare's day.

2 Study this image of Shakespeare's Globe, then draw a large plan of the stage with its two main entrances, small inner area and two supporting pillars.

   a On this plan, mark where you would place all the actors for the opening scene of the play.

   b Label the drawing, with a brief explanation for each of your choices.

The Globe Theatre has now been rebuilt very near the site of the original theatre. Many of the productions there are staged more or less as Shakespeare's audiences saw them.

IN MODERN THEATRE

Shakespeare often moves the action from place to place as he takes us from scene to scene. *Romeo and Juliet* therefore requires a set that can be adapted quickly and easily from one scene to another.

Apart from the requirements of the physical set, there is the question of where and when to locate the events. Virtually all modern editions contain stage directions giving precise, but basic, locations for each scene and sometimes instructions about what different characters are doing. Early editions did not have these stage directions. The Globe did not use lighting or scenery, and Shakespeare was involved in the earliest productions, so actors could ask him about how to interpret their characters. Today's directors and actors therefore have a lot of freedom because scripts tell us what the characters say, but the rest of the information has been added by later editors, not by William Shakespeare. From this point of view, it is not surprising that performances of the play can differ so much.

Some productions have based their set and costumes on designs suitable for the Italian city of Verona mentioned in Shakespeare's play. Others have relocated the story to different countries such as the Middle East or China – in fact, just about anywhere where there are rival factions engaged in a struggle.

Different productions have dressed the Montagues and Capulets as different races, different religions, different social classes and rival criminal gangs.

Each approach provides its own context in which the complex love of Romeo and Juliet can be explored.

KEY MOMENTS WHEN STAGING *ROMEO AND JULIET*

Here are some of the defining moments of the drama:

- The play begins with playful banter between the servants of the two households, which explodes into a fight.
- The Capulet ball (Act 1 Scene 5) is not only very colourful and grand; it is also the occasion where Romeo and Juliet meet and fall instantly in love. The moment they first set eyes on each other, and experience their first kiss, is very intense and powerful.
- Perhaps the best-known scene in the play has come to be known as 'the balcony scene'. Shakespeare himself never actually mentions the word 'balcony'! Some productions simply have Romeo standing in the Capulet orchard, looking up at Juliet's window. In other productions, the lovers' second meeting takes place in more unusual settings.
- The duel between Mercutio and Tybalt is a real turning point. It is another violent and electric moment and it marks the first deaths in the play. This is when Romeo becomes a killer and there is no way back for him. Some say this scene is the start of the **tragedy**.
- Finally, the ending of the play offers many interesting staging possibilities. Would you emphasise the terrible tragedy by having Juliet wake up before Romeo actually dies? Some 19th-century productions ended quite suddenly, with the death of Juliet, and cut the final part of Shakespeare's script. This was their way of underlining the importance of Juliet's death. Then there is the uncertainty of Montague and Capulet's words to each other, which close the play. Is their feud really over?

DEVELOP AND REVISE

1 Read through the play, noting each time that Shakespeare changes location.

- a   How many of these changes are there?
- b   What is their theatrical effect?

2 If you were directing *Romeo and Juliet*, where would you set the play?

- a   In what time period would it be set?
- b   What kind of groups would you make the Montagues and the Capulets?

3 Shakespeare never tells us how the Montagues and Capulets came to be in conflict. What effect does not knowing this have on directors, actors and audiences?

4 Take one of the five key moments described:

- a   How would you stage it?
- b   What kind of impression would you want to create on your audience?
- c   Add stage directions showing how you want lines to be delivered and any actions or effects that you would include for dramatic impact.

ROMEO AND JULIET: POPULAR AND ADAPTABLE

This play has always been very popular. It has been performed many times in every century since Shakespeare wrote it, and more recently it has been staged in countries around the world. Directors have sometimes adapted it to reflect the taste and fashion of their own time. For example one 18th-century production included an elaborate funeral procession and even extra **dialogue** between the lovers in the tomb.

Romeo and Juliet has been turned into operas, ballets, musicals, television series and films.

Two influential film versions of the play are those by directors Franco Zeffirelli (1968) and Baz Luhrmann (1996). Zeffirelli's film made powerful use of the contrast between the dark indoor world and the scorching heat of the outdoor scenes. The stone buildings and street locations were very atmospheric and realistic. This approach was echoed by a more recent film adaptation, directed by Carlo Carlei (2013).

Baz Luhrmann relocated the play to a fictional North American setting, Verona Beach. He modernised the action by including drug trips, car chases and gunfights. He also made use of a modern soundtrack to highlight the key themes of the play.

Clearly, a film-maker has many tools that are not available to theatre directors. For example a film-maker can add special effects or choose to have close-ups or wide-screen shots at key moments.

 Watch directors pitch their ideas for a new production on Cambridge Elevate.

DEVELOP AND REVISE

1 What aspects of the story of *Romeo and Juliet* do you think continue to appeal to an audience in the 21st century.

   a Jot down one key element on a sticky note and display it for other students to look at.

   b Pick out what you think are the most significant elements as the class members pool their ideas.

When people read novels, they often want to find out what happens next: for example in a whodunit, they want to know who committed the crime. In the case of *Romeo and Juliet*, most people already know what's going to happen and how it will end. Some audience members will have read the play and seen previous productions. But even for those who haven't, the opening Chorus gives us a plot summary: the quarrelling families, the lovers, their death and the fathers ending the quarrel.

2 How do you think this affects the audience's experience of watching a production?

3 There are many differences between film and stage productions. Find the differences listed in this unit and add some more of your own.

4 Which scenes in *Romeo and Juliet* do you think would work particularly well on film? Why?

 Explore the different ways the play can be set on Cambridge Elevate.

8

Character and characterisation

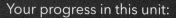

How does Shakespeare create such dramatic characters?

Your progress in this unit:

- understand and explore the characters in the play
- interpret how the characters represent ideas and attitudes
- explore the ways Shakespeare presents these characters
- analyse the changes in certain characters through the play
- write about character and characterisation.

CHARACTER OR CONSTRUCT?

In the past, critics treated characters in plays and novels as though they were real people:

- analysing their actions
- weighing up their good and bad points
- discussing whether a character's actions were believable and consistent
- asking, for example, whether Romeo and Juliet behaved and reacted the way real-life young people would respond.

Today's critics usually view characters as **constructs**. For example we could explore how Shakespeare presents Romeo as a young man in love, or as a tragic hero who contributes to the tragic outcome of the play.

Of course, if the lovers' story is to grip us, we have to feel emotionally involved with their experiences. When writing about characters for your exam, remember to focus on the characters as devices created by the writer – and not as real people.

MAJOR AND MINOR CHARACTERS

Editors of Shakespeare's plays often divide the characters into major characters and minor characters.

The major characters are the most important ones in the play. Obviously, they include Romeo and Juliet; many would argue that Friar Lawrence, the Nurse and Mercutio are also major characters.

Romeo

Romeo's first appearance in the play marks him out as a sad, unfulfilled young man who is given to walking alone and brooding. He believes he is in love with Rosaline. His character is changed by meeting Juliet. But, unlike her, he doesn't really grow out of his immaturity. He is devoted to Juliet, but he can act selfishly or without thinking, as when he kills Tybalt.

After seeking advice from Friar Lawrence, he breaks down and throws himself to the ground. How will an audience react to this, if they compare him to Juliet and how she deals with her challenges? He behaves recklessly again at the end as he races back to die with Juliet in the tomb. Do audiences regain respect for him when he shows his deep love for her in his long final speech? Do you think they feel renewed sympathy for him at this point?

> 🔑 **Key terms**
>
> **construct:** device that a playwright uses to examine key themes and ideas.

Juliet

Juliet is not introduced until the third scene of the play, long after we have met Romeo and many other male characters. She is very young (not yet fourteen) and has only seven lines to speak, in conversation with her mother and the Nurse, in her first scene.

Perhaps the most interesting aspect of Juliet's presentation is the speed at which she becomes a young woman. The turning point seems to be meeting Romeo. She impulsively kisses him and longs to be with him. Her shyness disappears in the 'balcony scene', where she speaks maturely and confidently, easily out-talking Romeo. She goes from strength to strength, arranging the marriage and going against her father's instructions. She has to deal with the way her parents abandon her and she shows courage in deciding to take the Friar's potion. Then, when she believes she will have to live without her beloved Romeo, she shows decisiveness in a different way by taking her own life.

Mercutio

Mercutio is a very complex character. He is perhaps best understood by thinking about the way he plays around with language, refusing to take life seriously. But he also has a dark side. Devoted to Romeo, he feels betrayed by Romeo's devotion to Juliet and his refusal to fight Tybalt. This brings out his violence and aggression.

Mercutio's dramatic role is key to understanding his part in the play:

- Mercutio's death in Act 3 is the first one in the play
- His death spurs Romeo to kill Tybalt and pushes the play towards its tragic end
- His attitude to love contrasts with Romeo's
- His heavily sexual joking characterises the 'male' world of the play
- His humour varies the tension, and relieves the intensity of the **tragedy**.

1 To study his dramatic role, take each of these five points in turn and consider the impact on the play if it was removed.

2 Now try the two-fold approach to exploring character with the Nurse and Friar Lawrence.

   a   Write a 'pen portrait' summarising their character in four or five sentences.
   b   Explore their specific role in the play.
   c   Compare your versions with those written by others.

DEVELOP AND REVISE

1 Look at the cast list at the front of the edition you're studying.

   a   Based on a quick recall of what happens in the play, which characters would you label 'major' and which 'minor'?
   b   How real is this distinction?

 Watch characters being interviewed in the hot seat on Cambridge Elevate.

2 Write the names of the 20 speaking parts in the play on individual slips of paper. Each person in the class takes one slip of paper at random.

a   Look through the play and find when your allotted character features in the action. Note down the act and scene, and what they **do** in it. (If you finish quickly, you can help collect information on one of the bigger characters.)

b   Then, based on the whole group's findings, discuss how to rank the characters in terms of their importance to the action of the play. Use a grid like this to organise your responses:

Character's name	The kind of things they do in the play	Why that makes them important	Possible rank order

3 If you repeat the exercise, looking at what (and how much) the characters **say** (rather than **do**), how different is the outcome? You could look at the topics they speak about, what they say about other characters, and the kind of language that is typically linked with them.

4 Adapt your 'actions' grid, changing your second column heading to 'The kind of things they say in the play'.

5 Afterwards, you could produce a whole class wall display, mapping how all the characters add to the action of *Romeo and Juliet* and some of their most memorable and important comments.

6 Draw a large outline of a gingerbread man (like this one) on a piece of sugar paper and use it to summarise a character, 'from the inside' and 'the outside'. We've completed a diagram for Benvolio, as an example.

a   Choose a character and write their name at the top.

b   **Inside** the outline of the figure, write what the character thinks about others and themselves.

c   **Outside** the outline, write what others think and feel about them.

Benvolio

Good friend to Romeo. Early on, he is concerned to find out the reasons for Romeo's sadness and lonely brooding.

Seen as a peacekeeper. Dislikes violence and tries to break up the quarrel in the opening scene. This makes Tybalt think he is a 'coward'.

7 Provide evidence from the text for all your ideas. As a class, you could complete the 'Role on the Wall' for each of the major characters and leave it up for display.

8 Study these two images of Romeo. Which do you think better matches your idea of Romeo?

9 Do the same with the two images of Juliet.

10 Look back closely at the parts of Romeo and Juliet in the play. Based on your investigations, produce a list of the kind of characteristics you would be looking for if you were casting these two roles in a production of the play.

11 Choose a scene, or a key part of a scene, that you think is important to understanding one of the major characters.

   a Copy out the most important things they say in that scene into a grid like the one shown for Juliet.

   b Explain how you would instruct the actor playing the role to deliver the lines.

What Juliet says on her first appearance in Act 1 Scene 3	How the actor should deliver the lines
'How now, who calls?'	In a playful mood? Almost childlike innocence and simplicity?

12 Find images (from newspapers or magazines) of famous actors or celebrities who you think would play the roles well. Explain your choices. As an extension, you could find several different images for Romeo and Juliet, reflecting how they show different sides of their personalities as the play progresses.

13 Choose a character and write (in **prose**) as though you were them. Take a key incident or episode in which your character is involved and retell it from their point of view. Aim to capture the way your character thinks and feels. You can include some of Shakespeare's own words.

9

Ideas, perspectives and themes

What big ideas dominate *Romeo and Juliet*?

Your progress in this unit:
- understand and explore the major ideas in the play
- interpret how these themes are communicated to an audience
- explore different interpretations and perspectives on the play
- explain the play's impact on you.

THEMES IN *ROMEO AND JULIET*

A **theme** is a central idea at the heart of a text: what a particular play, novel or poem is all about. In *Romeo and Juliet*, one of the main themes is falling in love, since the main plot follows the story of what happens to Romeo and Juliet after they fall in love and get married. However, the play has other themes too, including fate, revenge, family relationships and so on.

Shakespeare continually returned to themes that he found interesting, trying out different ways of looking at them. In virtually all his plays he explores themes that conflict with one another. In *Romeo and Juliet* he looks at the theme of love but its opposite (hate) also influences what happens. There are a number of powerful thematic oppositions at the heart of the play that help to create very exciting drama. It is possible to trace the development of each pair of opposed themes through the play, and to consider how each one contributes to the way events turn out at the end.

Light and darkness

The interplay of light and darkness is probably one of the most noticeable themes in *Romeo and Juliet*. It is often very strikingly explored in the way the play is staged in the theatre. If you look closely, you will see that Romeo and Juliet's love is frequently presented using attractive, positive images of light, as we might expect: torches, stars, gunpowder, fire, the sun. Unsurprisingly, Shakespeare uses images of night, clouds, churchyards, tombs and blackness to express the threat to the lovers' happiness.

Yet, interestingly, Juliet is excited by the darkness as she waits to meet Romeo on their wedding night. Perhaps the excitement comes from the risk they are taking. Or it could be that the darkness will hide her sexual awakening. She explores this idea in her **soliloquy** in Act 3 Scene 2.

The final scene takes place in the darkness of a funeral vault. Even here, Romeo draws attention to Juliet's dazzling presence. He thinks she makes **'This vault a feasting presence full of light.'** In his 1996 film version, Baz Lurhmann made sure that audiences noticed this by adorning the tomb with hundreds of brightly lit candles (see photo in Unit 5). Nevertheless, being a tragedy, the play still ends in darkness and death.

Fortune: the power of fate over individuals

Several times in the play, we are made to confront the question: who or what is to blame for Romeo and Juliet's deaths? While Shakespeare shows that the two young lovers' own choices and actions have affected the outcome, he also makes it clear that things beyond their control have shaped their lives. When the opening Chorus describes Romeo and Juliet as a **'pair of star-crossed lovers'**, he is talking about astrology: their fate was written in the stars (their horoscopes). As events move towards their tragic climax, Romeo defies fate: **'then I defy you, stars!'** By then it is too late.

Is this also part of the inevitable tragedy? Is Shakespeare saying that whatever humans do, they cannot predict what fate has in store for them and they cannot overcome it? Or do humans end up making things happen through their own foolish actions?

Romeo and Juliet are shown as young people who fear the future. Even before Romeo meets Juliet, he is full of anxiety about going to Capulet's party. He senses that something will go wrong. He has bad dreams (premonitions). Juliet also foresees bad things. On her final parting from Romeo, she has a frightening vision of him **'dead in the bottom of a tomb'**.

Completely chance events (things that no one plans or foresees) also have a big impact. For example Romeo ends up killing Tybalt when he is trying to make friends with him. Likewise, the Friar's well-meaning plan goes dreadfully wrong because his vital message is not delivered. Juliet wakes up in the tomb only **after** Romeo has drunk the poison.

Fathers and daughters

A key moment in *Romeo and Juliet* is when Capulet is enraged at his daughter's rejection of the marriage he has arranged for her. Lady Capulet is also furious and disowns her daughter: '**Do as thou wilt, for I have done with thee.**' You may feel that Juliet isn't being deliberately unreasonable. She has no romantic feelings for Paris so why should she be forced to marry him? Some productions help the audience sympathise with her by presenting Paris as an arrogant, bossy man with the same attitude as Capulet. In some productions her father not only verbally abuses her (which is in Shakespeare's script) but also hits her (which is the director's interpretation).

You should form your own opinion and show which aspects of the play have influenced that opinion. However, it is worth thinking about the original context as well. The play's first audiences would probably have sympathised with Juliet – but still agreed with Capulet. When Shakespeare was writing, it was expected that first fathers and then husbands would control girls' and women's lives. This may have been why Queen Elizabeth I (who ruled when this play was written) chose not to marry. Male power in the family was the equivalent of the king's power in the state. In this sense, Juliet's disobedience was revolutionary.

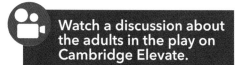

Watch a discussion about the adults in the play on Cambridge Elevate.

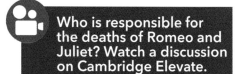

Who is responsible for the deaths of Romeo and Juliet? Watch a discussion on Cambridge Elevate.

Young and old, fast and slow

Romeo and Juliet are both young (Juliet is not yet fourteen) so it's not surprising that they are eager to embrace life. They make decisions quickly. At the start of the play, Romeo is in love with Rosaline. Yet very soon he has met and fallen in love with Juliet. By the end of the 'balcony scene', Juliet has promised to marry him, even though she knows it is against her father's wishes. When Romeo goes to visit Friar Lawrence, he is full of impatience. Seeing this, the Friar advises: **'Wisely and slow, they stumble that run fast'**.

As the play hurtles towards its conclusion, Shakespeare speeds up the action. After the violent deaths of Mercutio and Tybalt, the Friar has to move quickly with his plan. Juliet impulsively drinks his potion. Romeo hears news of her death and races back to Verona. In fact, the whole play takes place in only four days and Shakespeare shows us very clearly how the events fit into this time frame.

Thought and feeling

The lovers may be rushing foolishly, but the older characters are not necessarily any wiser. Romeo and Juliet are trapped in a web of hate spun by their elders. Shakespeare doesn't suggest that Lord and Lady Capulet are happily married. (In some productions, Lady Capulet is shown being very close to Tybalt.) Juliet's Nurse urges her to get over Romeo and marry Paris: does this show the Nurse stupidly failing to understand Juliet's feelings or wisely understanding the way life works? Friar Lawrence arrives too late to save Romeo and his attempt to persuade Juliet to leave with him fails: he is trying to argue logically when she is too full of emotion to listen. You could conclude that Juliet was let down by all the adults who should have protected her.

Love and hate, life and death

Romeo and Juliet's relationship of love is played out against a backdrop of hatred. The city of Verona is simmering with the enmity between the Montagues and Capulets even though no one remembers what began their feud. Romeo himself says **'Here's much to do with hate, but more with love'** in the opening scene.

The males, particularly the young males, spend much of their time swaggering and arguing. Tybalt would rather fight than talk. Mercutio sees Romeo backing down after Tybalt's challenge and feels he must fight to uphold his honour. Mercutio's language often bristles with insults. Both he and Capulet's servants joke about sex in aggressive ways. Capulet humiliates and verbally abuses his daughter. Romeo knows he risks the death penalty if he gets caught in Lord Capulet's grounds.

We know from the beginning that even though Romeo and Juliet are young and full of energy, they are both going to die. All their tender moments together are overshadowed by death. Perhaps Montague and Capulet make up their quarrel at the end, but they have paid for the truce with the lives of their children.

DEVELOP AND REVISE

1 How far do you control your own fate? Look at how fate works in *Romeo and Juliet*. Events such as Tybalt's death, the Friar's plan and the timing of Juliet's awakening in the tomb all drive the plot in different ways.

   a How does Shakespeare balance the impact of personal decisions against impersonal events?

   b In Act 3 Scene 1, Romeo calls himself **'fortune's fool'**. What does he mean by this?

2 How far do you think it is possible to have any sympathy for Lord and Lady Capulet? Look at how they behave towards Juliet throughout the play, then argue your case.

3 Take one of the themes outlined in this unit. Look through the play for evidence of how your chosen theme features in the text.

   a Show that evidence on a wall poster and display it on the classroom wall.

   b Decorate the poster with real-life images that fit your theme (taken from magazines or the Internet), then add your own comments and evaluations.

10

Language, form and structure in *Romeo and Juliet*

Why does the language in *Romeo and Juliet* have such an impact?

Your progress in this unit:
- analyse and explore language across the whole play
- explore and interpret links between character and language
- identify and analyse common images or features of language
- write about Shakespeare's use of language.

USE OF IMAGES

Several phrases from *Romeo and Juliet* have become part of our everyday language. Here are some examples:

- 'star-crossed lovers'
- 'a wild-goose chase'
- 'like lightning'
- 'parting is such sweet sorrow'
- 'what's in a name?'
- 'a plague o' both your houses!'
- 'a fool's paradise'.

Phrases like these have become part of the way we talk, because they use such colourful, memorable **imagery**. Images are word pictures. They are frequently based on comparing one thing with another, often in an unusual and thought-provoking way. Shakespeare uses three kinds of image in particular: **similes**, **metaphors** and **personification**.

Similes

Similes compare one thing to another using the word 'like' or 'as'. Romeo describes Juliet in Act 2 Scene 2: '**The brightness of her cheek would shame those stars, / As daylight doth a lamp**'. Romeo is describing Juliet's radiance. It is brighter than the stars, like the light of the sun ('**daylight**') compared to that of an artificial lamp.

Metaphors

Metaphors are also comparisons. But whereas a simile says one thing is **like** another, metaphors suggest that one thing **is the same as** something else. Therefore Romeo doesn't say that Juliet is **like** a '**bright angel**'; he says she **is** one.

Personification

Personification treats all types of things as though they were people, sometimes pretending they have human feelings or senses. Friar Lawrence therefore describes morning as '**grey-eyed**' and says it '**smiles**'. In Act 4 Scene 5, you will find Capulet using a powerful personification of death.

Repeated images

Shakespeare repeats key images in order to strengthen the main **themes** in the play. This helps the audience see links between several ideas on which the play is based. Some of these images also help to create character and to underline the difficult situation the two young lovers find themselves in.

For example there are many images about **light and darkness**. In Romeo's mind, Juliet is often linked with things that are bright or shining. After first seeing her, he says '**O she doth teach the torches to burn bright**'. As well as images of light, Romeo also uses words about the stars and heavens when he thinks about her. It is noticeable, too, that Juliet also speaks in such images when she thinks about Romeo: '**Take him and cut him out in little stars**' This use of language shows that they are connected. At a human level, they use similar images because they have similar personalities. At a deeper level, the shared imagery suggests that they are fated to fall in love: they have no choice in the matter.

Juliet is also linked with images of **death**, with the language often suggesting that Death is a person. Capulet says Death has become Juliet's husband: '**Death is my son-in-law, Death is my heir, / My daughter he hath wedded.**'

Romeo and Juliet's young love is also described in terms of **haste and speed**. Romeo says: '**I stand on sudden haste.**' In contrast, the older, wiser Friar tells Romeo to '**love moderately, long love doth so**'. In other words, if Romeo wants his love for Juliet to last, the Friar says his affection should not be so quick and reckless. He should take his time and let their love develop gradually.

Romeo and Juliet's love is described using many other images, which perhaps indicates how difficult it is to define precisely. For example it is compared to the moon when Juliet worries about it not lasting (because the moon changes size and shape and disappears once a month). At other points in the play, it is compared to gunpowder or the flash of lightning, a bud that hasn't yet flowered, or something as '**boundless**' as the sea.

CONFUSIONS AND CONTRADICTIONS

Oxymorons and antitheses

Shakespeare sometimes shows how complicated Romeo and Juliet's world is by using two other language devices: **oxymorons** and **antithesis**.

An oxymoron places two contradictory ideas side by side and fuses them together. Shakespeare gives Romeo lots of oxymorons when we first see him in the play. He sees love as '**feather of lead, bright smoke, cold fire, sick health**' and so on. When he has to leave Juliet at the end of the 'balcony scene' he says being away from her is '**such sweet sorrow**'.

Juliet also uses oxymorons to explore her own confused state of mind. When she discovers that Romeo has killed Tybalt, she struggles to understand how her beautiful Romeo could have committed such a horrible act. She speaks of Romeo using lots of oxymorons such as '**damnéd saint, an honourable villain**'. Continuing the idea of the lovers being linked by language, they both use oxymorons based on feathers.

Key terms

simile: an imaginative comparison or an image that uses 'like' or 'as'.

metaphor: an image or imaginative comparison in which one thing is said to be another.

oxymoron: a phrase containing a contradiction.

An antithesis places two (or sometimes more) ideas next to one another so as to draw attention to the contrast between them. Antitheses can act like tiny discussions, giving you two sides of an argument. When Juliet first learns who Romeo is, she declares '**My only love sprung from my only hate**'. Antitheses are important throughout the play. The opening Chorus brings together '**ancient grudge**' with '**new mutiny**', '**civil blood**' and '**civil hands**', '**fearful passage of their death-marked love**' with '**the continuance of the parents' rage**'.

Oxymorons and antitheses depend on a pair of opposed words or phrases. They are an important aspect of a drama about pairs: '**Two households**' and '**a pair of star-crossed lovers**'. They also dramatise the complexity of some decisions.

Romeo senses the gathering problems he and Juliet face even as they celebrate their wedding. He says: '**More light and light, more dark and dark our woes**'.

Puns

A **pun** is a joke based on two or more words that sound similar but have different meanings (homophones). Shakespeare uses puns in all his plays, including his tragedies. They help create the lighter moments in *Romeo and Juliet*, such as scenes with the Nurse or Mercutio. These two characters do not take life, love or death as seriously as the two lovers. They can be funny, rude and openly sexual, though modern audiences can't always understand their jokes. For example when Mercutio says '**medlar**', the 16th-century audiences would have known that the word meant a type of fruit like an apple, but it was also slang for a woman's sexual organs. Even when Mercutio is dying, he makes puns: his last words in Act 3 Scene 1 include a simile, an antithesis – and a pun.

Puns may seem a very minor aspect of the play but (like oxymorons, similes, metaphors and antitheses) they also depend on pairs of words. They are therefore an equally important part of the drama of love and conflict.

VERSE AND PROSE

Most of the play is written in **blank verse iambic pentameters**. This is a type of poetry that Shakespeare used all through his career:

- Blank verse – it has no **rhyme**.
- Pentameters – there are **five strong syllables** in each line (just as a pentagon has five sides). The lines are usually ten syllables long.
- Iambic – the strong syllables alternate with weak ones, in the order *weak–strong* (dee-*dum*, dee-*dum*). Shakespeare takes this underlying rhythmic pattern and then varies it continually so that it doesn't become predictable.

Romeo and Juliet also has passages in rhyming verse and in prose. When the Prince says: '**Bear hence his body, and attend our will: / Mercy but murders, pardoning those that kill**' he is using a rhyming couplet, when two lines end with words that sound the same. If you study the Chorus's Prologue, you will see that it is a sonnet, a type of rhyming poem.

Shakespeare's higher-status characters (such as the Prince, Capulet and Montague) tend to speak verse. His lower-status characters (for example the servants and the Nurse) usually speak prose. But this is not an unbreakable rule. The Nurse speaks verse when she is talking to Juliet, perhaps to show that she is still an authority figure in Juliet's life. Equally, Romeo, Mercutio and Benvolio all speak prose sometimes. Prose is often the language of the comic scenes, but just as he dies with a pun, so Mercutio dies using (highly decorative) prose.

1 Look through the play for ways in which Shakespeare uses images of light, death and speed to present the relationship between Romeo and Juliet.

   a   Draw pictures of one or two of the most striking examples you come across.

   b   Label them with the appropriate words from the text.

2 Look through Act 1 Scene 1 to see how anger, violence and hatred are expressed. The latter part of the same scene shows Romeo discussing his love for Rosaline. How does his speech there differ from his speech when he first begins to talk about being in love with Juliet?

3 Take any scene and list the examples of metaphors, similes, personification and so on.

   a   How do the images work?

   b   What ideas does each image involve?

4 Look at the role of rhyme in the play – for example the use of rhyming couplets to end scenes and acts. Study the pattern of rhymes in the Chorus's Prologue to the play and his return between Acts 1 and 2. After noticing the pattern, turn to Act 1 Scene 5 and look for a sonnet there, created by Romeo and Juliet's dialogue.

   a   What are the key images in that sonnet?

   b   Why do you think Shakespeare has the two lovers share the words of a sonnet in such a way?

Key terms

pun: a 'play on words'; the use of a word or phrase with a double meaning.

homophone: a word that is pronounced the same as another word but has a different meaning.

slang: informal language.

Preparing for your exam

Your progress in this unit:
- understand what the exam requires and the skills you need to show
- prepare for your exam by planning and responding to a practice question
- assess your skills against example responses to the question
- improve your skills in writing for GCSE English Literature.

Romeo and Juliet is assessed in your GCSE English Literature Paper 1 examination, in **Section A** of **Paper 1: Shakespeare and the 19th-century novel**. Paper 1 lasts for 1 hour and 45 minutes and is worth 40% of your GCSE in English Literature. You have just over 50 minutes for your answer on *Romeo and Juliet*.

You will have to answer **one** question on *Romeo and Juliet*. You will be required to write in detail about an extract from the play that is printed on your exam paper and then to write about the play as a whole. There are 30 marks for this question. There are also 4 marks available for assessment objective 4 on this question.

The assessment objective skills

For this Section A question, your answers will be assessed against four assessment objectives (AOs) – skills that you are expected to show. Notice the marks for each AO and take account of this as you manage your time and focus your response.

AO1: Read, understand and write about what happens in the play, referring to the text and using relevant quotations. (12 marks)

AO2: Analyse the language, form and structure used by Shakespeare to create meanings and effects. (12 marks)

AO3: Show an understanding of the context of the play. (6 marks)

The 'contexts' of AO3 might include when Shakespeare wrote the play, the period in which he set the play and why, and the context of different audiences, including you in the 21st century.

AO4: Use a range of vocabulary and sentence structures for clarity, purpose and effect, with accurate spelling and punctuation. (4 marks)

What to do in the exam

- At the beginning of the exam, spend some time looking very carefully at the question. Make sure you understand exactly what you are being asked to do.
- Annotate the extract and plan what you want to write about for the extract and about the play as a whole.

Planning and responding to a question

You can use this example question to help you prepare and practise your skills for the exam. The following pages will help you to assess your skills so that you know what you do well and can focus on areas to improve.

Read the following extract from Act 1 Scene 2 of **Romeo and Juliet** and then use the skills you have developed to answer the question that follows. At this point in the play, Lord Capulet and Paris are discussing Juliet.

request: but for what? Shakespeare keeps audience in suspense

makes her sound naive and too young to be married

she's caught between childhood and adulthood; birthday is important – the day before the Harvest Festival

children

do rhyming couplets create a more romantic atmosphere?

PARIS

5   And pity 'tis, you lived at odds so long.
     But now, my lord, what say you to my suit?

CAPULET

     But saying o'er what I have said before:
     My child is yet a stranger in the world,
     She hath not seen the change of fourteen years;
     Let two more summers wither in their pride,
10   Ere we may think her ripe to be a bride.

PARIS

     Younger than she are happy mothers made.

CAPULET

     And too soon marred are those so early made.
     Earth hath swallowed all my hopes but she;
15   She's the hopeful lady of my earth.
     But woo her, gentle Paris, get her heart,
     My will to her consent is but a part;
     And she agreed, within her scope of choice
     Lies my consent and fair according voice.

she's only 13; girls of this age did get married in Shakespeare's time but it was rare.

image of age and decay

alliteration of soft sounds

repetition; a possible pun on 'maid'

has had other children but only Juliet remains so she will become a rich woman when he dies; it is starting to look like a trade-off – a marriage between two rich families

this is so important to him; later in the play his will changes

Starting with this conversation, explain how far you think Shakespeare presents Lord Capulet as a good father. Write about:

- how Shakespeare presents Lord Capulet in this extract
- how Shakespeare presents Lord Capulet in the play as a whole.

[30 marks]

AO4 [4 marks]

Plan your answer

When planning your answer to any question, focus on three key areas:

- What do you know about the characters, events and ideas at this stage in this extract, and in the play as a whole? (AO1)
- What comments can you make about how Shakespeare uses language and style, using examples from this extract? (AO2)
- What is relevant in this extract that relates to the context of the play as a whole? (AO3)

Look at this example of a student's plan. Then explore the example paragraphs and development of skills in writing for GCSE English Literature that follow.

Remember:

- The **best answers** will explore Shakespeare's craft and purpose in creating a character. They will connect what the character does to the writer's ideas and to the effects upon an audience watching. They offer a personal response and provide many well-explained details.
- **Good answers** will show a clear understanding of how Shakespeare develops Lord Capulet, using well-chosen examples.
- **Weaker answers** will only explain what happens with Lord Capulet, without using many examples or mentioning how Shakespeare presents him.

Show your skills

It may help you to look at these five example paragraphs and the development of skills shown in writing about *Romeo and Juliet*, to develop your own writing.

Paris wants to marry Juliet and asks Lord Capulet if he can. Lord Capulet tells him to wait for two years.

> some simple facts stated

Paris wants to marry Juliet ('what say you to my suit?') and asks Lord Capulet if he can. Lord Capulet tells him to wait because she is only thirteen and so is too young to be married.

> statement supported with quotation

Shakespeare gives Lord Capulet the line 'My child is yet a stranger in the world'. This may just mean that she doesn't get out much but it probably means that she is still very innocent and does not know how adults behave. However, young girls of this age were sometimes brides in Shakespeare's times, when the legal age for marriage was 12 years old for girls. Later in the play her mother tells Juliet that she herself was a young bride.

> provides a range of detail to keep clearly illustrating a point

When Shakespeare describes Juliet as being 'yet a stranger in the world' he is emphasising her innocence and naivety as well as her age. The word 'world' is used later in the play. For Friar Lawrence 'the world is broad and wide' and may well hold somewhere where Romeo and Juliet can find happiness. On the other hand, Romeo tells the Apothecary 'The world is not thy friend'. The world will not be a friend to the lovers; perhaps it would have been better if Juliet had remained a stranger to it.

> uses details to develop an interpretation going beyond what the text states explicitly

There is an interesting contrast between the words 'wither' and 'ripe'. Shakespeare contrasts the decay of the natural world withering and becoming dead for the winter with the ripeness of the spring. The word 'ripe' makes Juliet seem sexually attractive. Lord Capulet seems to be tempting Paris with thoughts of her virginity. This is why Shakespeare names her birthday as Lammas Eve, the end of the growth of spring and summer and the day before the harvest begins. It is almost as if Shakespeare were suggesting that Juliet was ready to enter a sexual relationship (or be harvested). This seems a particularly unpleasant image, given her age. The beautiful young girl on stage may seem to the audience to be a sacrifice to her father's greed.

> an argued interpretation focused on author, theatrical context and ideas

Plan and write your own response

Now plan and write your own response to the practice question about the conversation between Capulet and Paris. You can then assess your skills against the example responses that follow.

Assessing your skills using sample responses

The following extracts are from responses to the exam practice question you have already looked at. They show examples of skills at different levels when writing for GCSE English Literature. Use these examples to assess your own skills in responding to the practice question so that you know what you do well and can focus on areas to improve.

Compare these extracts with your own answer to the exam practice question. As you read the extracts, think about how far each example – and your own answer – is successful in:

* using details from the text to support what the students have written
* using details to build up an interpretation of a character or a theme
* exploring Shakespeare's use of language and structure as well as his intentions in writing the text.

Student A

This is taken from early in Student A's response:

The scene starts with a question from Paris. The audience would understand that he has already asked Lord Capulet if he can marry Juliet and Lord Capulet may have put off giving him a straight answer. It seems as if Lord Capulet is a really kind and caring father. He says that Juliet is still very young when he says 'She hath not seen the change of fourteen years'. This shows that he cares for her because he knows how old she is. He asks Paris to wait for another two years before he marries her. Paris replies that she is old enough to be married even though she is only thirteen! He says that even younger girls are happily married. This was the way that girls were treated at the time. Lord Capulet is not impressed with this and says that many girls who marry so young are unhappy. This would make the audience think that he was really concerned for his daughter's happiness. He wants what is best for her. But he does give Paris some hope by saying that he will agree if Juliet says that she loves him. This shows that he is a really good father who only wants what is best for his daughter.

> shows understanding of implicit meaning

> useful quotation from the text

> a judgement on his response

> textual reference but with no real explanation

> some context in Elizabethan England or Verona or both?

This is taken from further on in Student A's response:

In Act 3 Scene 5, Lord Capulet shows that he is a really bad father. He is cruel and unkind. For example he uses a long list to torment Juliet: 'Day, night, work, play, / Alone, in company'. Here he is shouting at Juliet to tell her just how hard he has tried to find her a suitable husband. In fact he hasn't tried at all.

> comment on reference.

> repeats the point but makes a case for him being a good father

Paris asked him first. Some of the elements in this list, like 'Day, night', are contrasts to show how hard he has tried. He then imitates his own daughter, 'I'll not wed'. The audience would think that this is a terrible thing to do to your own daughter. He then makes things even worse by saying that he will not care whether she starves or dies. Right at the end he lets something slip so that the audience understands why he is so angry. The real reason why he wants Juliet to marry Paris is that he has promised that she will, and he cannot bring himself to break his promise.

In the first paragraph Student A has shown the following skills and achievements:

- a good level of understanding of what happens in the dialogue
- use of one direct quotation with a comment on it
- use of several direct references to the text – using these to come to a judgement that the question has asked for
- an awareness of the audience
- starting to sustain the idea of Lord Capulet as a good father at the end of the paragraph even though there is a repetition of the idea
- the paragraph links to the question.

Working in a pair, annotate the second and third paragraphs of Student A's answer to see if you can find more examples of the same skills or any new ones.

What do you think is good about the answer?

Look carefully at the first three assessment objectives at the start of this section. What advice would you give Student A on how to improve this answer?

Student B

This is taken from early in Student B's response:

At first sight it appears that Shakespeare presents Lord Capulet as being a good, caring father. Because Juliet is his only child he wants to take care of her and make sure that she is happily married. If she doesn't want to marry Paris then Lord Capulet says that he will not make her. However, it might be rather different. Lord Capulet and Paris have obviously talked about Juliet before and Lord Capulet may be trying to make Juliet seem more attractive. Mentioning her very young age and the fact that she is 'a stranger to the world' (therefore very innocent) might make her all the more desirable. Shakespeare's use of the word 'ripe' has sexual connotations: she is ready to be enjoyed sexually. Shakespeare also adds the important detail that Juliet is Capulet's only surviving child. This is not to make the audience feel sorry for him as a grieving father or her as an only child. It is significant because at the time children and not wives inherited. When Capulet dies, Juliet will inherit all his land and money. This will, presumably, make her all the more attractive to Paris. The marriage would therefore mean the two families joining each other socially and, in time, financially. Rather than being a good father, Shakespeare may be presenting Lord Capulet as a scheming man who is ready to use his daughter to further his own ends and who discusses her as if she were a possession or a financial asset.

shows that Lord Capulet is a dramatic construct and not a real person

useful textual reference

prepares for an alternative interpretation

places extract in context

sustained comment on textual detail

interprets character with understanding of context

clear understanding of characterisation

alternative interpretation explored

This is taken from further on in Student B's response:

At the end of the play Shakespeare apparently presents Capulet as a distraught father grieving the loss of his child. It seems as if the promise made in The Prologue that the deaths will 'bury their parents' strife' will come about. It is interesting that Shakespeare uses the image of burial so early in the play in a clear indication of both the actions and the language to come.

Capulet even offers to shake Montague's hand. That said, there may be another interpretation. Shakespeare uses the technical word 'jointure' meaning money given at a wedding by the groom's father to the bride's father: a sort of cash payment for a woman. Even in his grief Capulet's first thought seems to be of money. He states that he cannot 'demand' anything other than a handshake, implying that he has given the matter some thought. He and Montague then involve themselves in an extravagant show of mourning. Each promises the other a golden statue. Again grief seems to be measured in terms of money with each trying to show he is as wealthy as the other. Shakespeare presents an ending that is not wholly convincing. The audience may not believe that the peace in Verona will be permanent.

This is a stronger response than Student A's. Student B is clearly focused on the author's craft and purpose, and on the text as drama.

The response engages with Shakespeare's use of language and characterisation. It develops ideas about Lord Capulet's views on the marriage of Juliet to Paris and the benefits this may bring him. It includes personal interpretation. It shows:

- understanding of Shakespeare's characterisation of Lord Capulet
- sustained comment on the meaning of textual details
- awareness of effects on the stage and on the audience when it is revealed that Juliet is his only surviving daughter
- some exploration of feelings and motives
- effective use of textual detail in stage directions and speech
- a developed consideration of Lord Capulet as a good/scheming father.

Working in a pair, annotate the second paragraph of Student B's answer to see if you can find more examples of the same skills or any new ones.

What do you think is good about Student B's answer?

Look carefully at the first three assessment objectives at the start of this section. What advice would you give Student B on how to improve this answer?

Student C

This is taken from the opening of Student C's response:

This extract not only shows the difference between men and women and old and young in the society of the time, in terms of the play's structure it also leads directly to the first meeting of Romeo and Juliet.

> begins to consider power of men and powerlessness of women

As the extract begins, two men are discussing the future of a young woman. She is not only silent but completely absent. The men have clearly had previous discussions on the same topic: how one man will give a young woman to another man as if she were an object, a present or a means for Lord Capulet to advance himself by becoming associated with Paris's family. Juliet herself has no say in her future. Even though Paris appears to defer to Capulet, calling him 'my lord', it is obvious to the audience that it is Paris who is the social and financial superior. Any association with his family would make the Capulet family even more powerful.

> Juliet is an object to be sold for gain

> good use of short quotation

> explains effect on audience

Capulet may pretend to consider Juliet's wishes when he claims, 'My will to her consent is but a part' but the words 'My will' leave the audience in no doubt that his will takes priority. The influence of parents, who are themselves subject to the influence of family and society as a whole, will lead to the tragic deaths.

> mixture of concept of power and Capulet's motivation

When Capulet says 'within her scope of choice' there is a clear implication that this scope will be severely limited. The final line of the extract has an echo of 'My will' in 'my consent'. Shakespeare presents a man convinced of his own power and importance: the idea that his daughter could possibly disobey his 'will' is not something he could ever imagine.

> summarises characterisation

> looks forward to rest of text

This is the best of the three student responses. When you have read this answer, comment on the ways in which Student C:

- understands what the extract is about – its ideas and its importance in the play as a whole
- explains the effect of the extract on an audience and shows why it has that effect
- uses quotations from the extract as evidence to support an argument and doesn't just put forward opinions without any support
- looks at the whole extract and doesn't get stuck on one part of it
- writes clearly and correctly
- convincingly explores and evaluates one or more of the ideas in the text as a whole.

Use what you have learned from this section to focus on skills to improve for your exam.

Practice questions

Use your learning in this section to create practice questions and develop your skills further.

1 Work with another student to:

- choose a topic from the list in this section, or a topic of your choice
- choose a suitable extract of around 300 words
- create your own practice questions.

You could use the format of the question in this section. Starting with the conversation between Lord Capulet and Paris, explain to what extent you think Shakespeare presents Lord Capulet as a good father.

Write about:

- how Shakespeare presents Lord Capulet in this particular extract
- how Shakespeare presents Lord Capulet in the play as a whole.

Use these prompts to create your question:

- Choose a suitable extract
- Choose a suitable topic
- Choose a focus for writing about the extract.

Your question should look like this:

Starting with this extract, write about how Shakespeare presents your choice of topic.

- **how Shakespeare presents your choice of focus in this extract**
- **how Shakespeare presents your choice of topic in the play as a whole.**

You could choose from the following themes, which Shakespeare explores in the play.

- dreams and realities
- loyalty to the family or group
- money versus love
- a major character
- a minor character
- children and adults
- marriages – good and bad
- how fate governs people's lives.

3 Now answer the question, using the skills you have developed.

As you plan and write, think about how you can show:

- a consistent focus on the question you have been asked, always remembering never to just retell the plot
- your knowledge of the details of the play by using direct quotations or references to the text if you cannot remember the quotations
- your understanding of a character or a setting or a theme
- your understanding of how Shakespeare has used language and structure to create the play
- your ideas about the context in which the play was written and how an audience in the 21st century might react to it.

4 Swap work with your partner. Using these points and your work in this section, comment on the skills shown in the answer. Suggest three areas that could be improved.

Remember that it is quite all right to say 'This might mean' or 'This may imply'. You are exploring the play, its characters, language and ideas, not conquering them.

Glossary

adjective a word that describes a noun

antithesis two opposite ideas that are put together to achieve a contrasting effect

blank verse unrhymed verse with carefully placed stressed and unstressed syllables

characterisation the way a writer paints a picture of a particular character, through their words, actions and reactions

connotation an idea or a feeling linked to the main meaning of a word – what it implies or suggests in addition to its literal meaning

construct device that a playwright uses to examine key themes and ideas

couplet a unit of two lines of poetry, often used in 'rhyming couplet'

dialogue a conversation between two or more people in a piece of writing

dramatic irony when the audience knows something about a character or plot that a character on stage is not aware of

foreshadow hint at what lies ahead

groundlings poorer audience members who stood on the ground around the stage, in Shakespeare's time

homophone a word that is pronounced the same as another word but has a different meaning

iambic pentameter the rhythm created by a line of ten syllables with five stressed syllables

imagery language intended to conjure up a vivid picture in the reader or audience's mind

juxtaposition the placement of two ideas or things near each other to invite comparison or contrast

metaphor an image or imaginative comparison in which one thing is said to be another

myth an ancient, traditional story, often about early history and sometimes involving magic

oxymoron a phrase containing a contradiction

personification the poetic device of giving human qualities to an object

poetic device a technique used by a writer, such as personification

props 'properties'; objects and items that help to set the scene in a play

prose writing that follows the style of normal speech

protagonist the central character in a play, film or book

pun a 'play on words'; the use of a word or phrase with a double meaning

rhyme scheme the pattern of a poem's rhyme, often identified by letters such as ABAB

simile an imaginative comparison or an image that uses 'like' or 'as'

slang informal language

soliloquy a long speech given by a character, usually alone on stage, as if they are thinking aloud

sonnet a poem of 14 lines with a distinctive rhyme scheme

theme an idea or concept that recurs throughout a play

tragedy a play with an unhappy ending, usually involving the downfall of the main character

verse writing that has a particular rhyme, pattern or rhythm

Acknowledgements

Picture credits

p. 5 Donald Cooper/Photostage; p. 6 Donald Cooper/Photostage; p. 7 Donald Cooper/Photostage; p. 8 Donald Cooper/Photostage; p. 10 Donald Cooper/Photostage; p. 14 Donald Cooper/Photostage; p. 15 Donald Cooper/Photostage; p. 16 Cooper/Photostage; p. 19 Donald Cooper/Photostage; p. 20 Donald Cooper/Photostage; p. 21 Donald Cooper/Photostage; p. 22 Donald Cooper/Photostage; p. 24 Donald Cooper/Photostage; p. 26 Donald Cooper/Photostage; p.27 Donald Cooper/Photostage; p. 28 (t) Donald Cooper/Photostage; p. 28 (b) outcast85/Thinkstock; p. 29 Donald Cooper/Photostage; p. 30 Donald Cooper/Photostage; p. 31 Donald Cooper/Photostage; p. 32 Donald Cooper/Photostage; p. 33 Donald Cooper/Photostage; p. 35 Donald Cooper/Photostage; p. 36 Donald Cooper/Photostage; p. 37 Donald Cooper/Photostage; p. 38 Donald Cooper/Photostage; p. 39 Donald Cooper/Photostage; p. 40 Donald Cooper/Photostage; p. 42 Donald Cooper/Photostage; p. 43 Donald Cooper/Photostage; p. 44 Elliott Franks/ArenaPAL; p. 49 Paramount/The Kobal Collection; p. 50 Donald Cooper/Photostage; p. 51 Donald Cooper/Photostage; p. 52 Donald Cooper/Photostage; p. 53 Donald Cooper/Photostage; p. 54 Donald Cooper/Photostage; p. 57 Donald Cooper/Photostage; p. 59 (t) Donald Cooper/Photostage; p. 59 (b) Donald Cooper/Photostage; p. 60 Donald Cooper/Photostage; p. 62 Donald Cooper/Photostage; p. 63 Donald Cooper/Photostage; p. 64 Donald Cooper/Photostage;

p. 65 Donald Cooper/Photostage; p. 67 (l) 20th Century Fox/The Kobal Collection; p. 67 (r) Paramount/The Kobal Collection; p.68 Geraint Lewis; p. 71 Donald Cooper/Photostage; p. 72 Donald Cooper/Photostage; p. 73 hipproductions/Thinkstock; p. 74 Donald Cooper/Photostage; p. 76 Donald Cooper/Photostage; p. 77 Donald Cooper/Photostage; p. 78 Donald Cooper/Photostage; p. 79 (t) The Granger Collection/Topfoto; p. 79 (b) Donald Cooper/Photostage; p. 81 20th Century Fox/The Kobal Collection; p. 82 Geraint Lewis; p. 85 (bl) Donald Cooper/Photostage; p. 85 Donald Cooper/Photostage; p. 85 (tl) Geraint Lewis; p.85 (tr) Donald Cooper/Photostage; p. 86 (t) Donald Cooper/Photostage; p.86 (b) Donald Cooper/Photostage; p. 87 Donald Cooper/Photostage; p. 88 (b) Elliott Franks/ArenaPAL; p. 88 (t) Donald Cooper/Photostage; p. 90 (t) Donald Cooper/Photostage; p. 90 (b) Donald Cooper/Photostage; p. 92 Donald Cooper/Photostage; p. 94 Donald Cooper/Photostage.

With thanks to Lucien Jenkins and Rob Smith.

Produced for Cambridge University Press by

White-Thomson Publishing
www.wtpub.co.uk

Editor: Kelly Davis
Designer: Tracey Camden